**INVISIBLE UNIVERSITY
FOR UKRAINE**

McCourtney Institute for Democracy

The Pennsylvania State University's McCourtney Institute for Democracy (http://democracyinstitute.la.psu.edu) was founded in 2012 as an interdisciplinary center for research, teaching, and outreach on democracy. The institute coordinates innovative programs and projects in collaboration with the Center for American Political Responsiveness and the Center for Democratic Deliberation.

Laurence and Lynne Brown Democracy Medal

The Laurence and Lynne Brown Democracy Medal recognizes outstanding individuals, groups, and organizations that produce exceptional innovations to further democracy in the United States or around the world. In even-numbered years, the medal spotlights practical innovations, such as new institutions, laws, technologies, or movements that advance the cause of democracy. Awards given in odd-numbered years highlight advances in democratic theory that enrich philosophical conceptions of democracy or empirical models of democratic behavior, institutions, or systems.

INVISIBLE UNIVERSITY FOR UKRAINE

ESSAYS ON DEMOCRACY AT WAR

EDITED BY OSTAP SEREDA,
BALÁZS TRENCSÉNYI,
TETIANA ZEMLIAKOVA, AND
GUILLAUME LANCEREAU

CORNELL UNIVERSITY PRESS
Ithaca and London

Thanks to generous funding from the McCourtney Institute for Democracy at Pennsylvania State University, the ebook editions of this book are available as open access volumes through the Cornell Open initiative.

First published 2024 by Cornell University Press

Librarians: A CIP catalog record for this book is available from the Library of Congress.

Library of Congress Control Number: 2024945865

ISBN 978-1-5017-8286-2 (paperback)
ISBN 978-1-5017-8287-9 (epub)
ISBN 978-1-5017-8288-6 (pdf)

Contents

INVISIBLE UNIVERSITY
FOR UKRAINE

Introduction

Power Banks of Democracy

OSTAP SEREDA AND BALÁZS TRENCSÉNYI

Laptops in Candlelight

In the autumn of 2022, Russian missiles began to target the Ukrainian power grid systematically, and the resulting outages handicapped most activities during the afternoons and evenings in all major Ukrainian cities. Even though mild weather decreased the danger of freezing, the paralyzing effect of unexpected power cuts was hard to bear. It put at risk numerous connections that were only recently reestablished through channels of virtual communication inside and outside the country after the first months of intensive fighting and destruction. The power cuts also threatened our online classes at the Invisible University for Ukraine (IUFU; https://www.ceu.edu/non-degree/Invisible-University), an international program of academic solidarity launched immediately after the full-scale Russian invasion.

Our classes usually began around 6 p.m. local time, letting students participate fully in the regular online or offline activities at their home universities. We were cautious not to duplicate programs offered within the Ukrainian educational system but to help its regeneration. Starting in April 2022 with 130 students and four courses in the humanities and social sciences, by the fall semester, IUFU offered seven courses for 350 Ukrainian students representing all major university centers in the country. As a rule, each class was cotaught every week by different instructors, invited from international and Ukrainian academic institutions. Classes were planned for a hundred minutes each, but we always stayed online longer; students patiently waiting for their turn to contribute to a debate or to confront a prominent scholar with their questions. We had agreed that if the air-raid alarms began in any student's locality, they should disconnect and watch the class recording later, but the frequent power cuts added another complication.

Fortunately, many students could rely on the newly acquired power banks to sustain their internet connections and laptop batteries. Even when rooms went dark, the light from the laptop screens continued to illuminate students' faces. Sometimes we even saw candles around the laptop. The Ukrainian lecturers had to be inventive too, searching for the right spot with an uninterrupted internet connection, often teaching from a bomb shelter. But the dynamic and often heated discussions continued.

Our students bore heavy traumas stemming from what they or their loved ones suffered. Among the organizers, we frequently debated whether our responsibility was to provide a haven away from the terrible realities of war, to avoid triggering students, or whether we should address war openly and intensively. Were we to follow the latter option, how would we deal with the sensitive and difficult topics, all the issues that are *не на часі* (not in time)? How to combine the reflective self-irony of academic discourse on the one hand and the terrifying dichotomies of war realities on the other? How to deal with emotions in a purportedly "rational" academic setting? We did not have easy answers to these questions, but we kept believing in the power of open discussion and hoped to empower our students with the tools of critical analysis and an informed scholarly approach.

The questions that we have been debating in the virtual classroom and during the summer and winter schools merged academic and existential aspects. How to deal with the Russian imperial and Soviet heritages? How to process the plethora of digital traces of the war? How to rebuild the cities destroyed by the Russian occupiers? How to represent the polyphony of Ukrainian culture internationally? How to preserve democratic institutions during a wartime state of emergency?

A central aim of IUFU became sustaining a pluralistic and democratic political and intellectual culture in Ukraine—bringing students with diverse life stories, linguistic and cultural practices, and political views into a common, welcoming space. A place where they could articulate differences but develop mechanisms of constructive argument. Likewise, many IUFU classes reflected on the ways to preserve and relaunch democratic government during and after the war. Guest speakers like the Nobel laureate human rights activist Oleksandra Matviichuk, or the European Union's anticorruption prosecutor Laura Codruța Kövesi, reminded the students that democracy is not a given but requires constant efforts and engagement.

Background: Returning to the "Questions Themselves"

Writing on what she called a crisis in education, Hannah Arendt stresses that crises offer a window of opportunity for posing the right questions, forcing us "back to the questions themselves" and requiring "from us either new or old answers, but in any case direct judgments."[1]

Reflecting on the prehistory of the Invisible University for Ukraine, it is important to note that it originates long before the full-scale invasion of Ukraine by Russian troops in February 2022. The need for uncommon institutional responses to the autocratic pressure on higher education has been a recurrent topic of discussion since the late 2000s. Throughout Central, Eastern, and Southeastern Europe, it had become obvious that successful convergence with an idealized "Western" model was an increasingly problematic aspiration. Democratic backsliding was partly to blame, but there were also growing doubts about the relevance of this classical "Western" academic model in the present.

Until recently, the violation of academic freedom has been conveniently localized in the Global South and Eastern Europe. China, India, Turkey, Russia, Belarus, and Hungary provided spectacular examples. However, universities are primary battlegrounds of the raging culture wars across the Western hemisphere right now, and it has become increasingly difficult to draw a straight line between the "free" and "unfree" worlds. Educational institutions are targets of autocratic regimes but are also under pressure in societies that otherwise still qualify as liberal democracies. Universities are now often perceived as hindrances to the free market logic, derailing the youth from taking up more socially and economically "useful" practical professions, or simply fostering an overly critical spirit toward the political establishment, while the contestation around free speech on campus surfaced the radical ideological polarization of these societies.

The case of the Central European University (CEU) is illustrative in many respects. Founded by the Hungarian-American philanthropist George Soros, CEU has been a flagship institution of the democratic transition in the region. In 2019 it relocated its US-accredited, degree-granting educational programs from Budapest to Vienna after Viktor Orbán's government orchestrated a hate campaign against

Soros and passed a new law explicitly targeting the university. CEU's departure indicated a failure of local and transnational institutions (including the European Union) to defend a university from a government embracing a vision of "illiberal democracy."[2]

Reflecting on such defeats is crucial when one seeks to defend the intellectual plurality and moral integrity of academic institutions under siege. These battles happen locally but ripple far beyond the originating country. As Bertolt Brecht reminds us, "The world is not obliged to be sentimental. Defeats should be acknowledged; but one should not conclude from them that there should be no more struggles."[3] IUFU drew its founding lessons from such traumatic experiences.

This response was also linked to the growing tension between three modes that together characterize modern academia: research, teaching, and public engagement. This model was rooted in the Humboldtian tradition, reconfigured in the mid-twentieth century during the trans-Atlantic exchange between American and European scholars and institutions, often mediated by "scholars at risk" escaping from totalitarian regimes. The autonomy of the university, let alone of research, was never perfect, even in the so-called West. But there was a dialogical relationship between academics and society characterizing post–World War II North America and Western Europe, and in this framework, the three modes could mutually reinforce each other. However, this model showed its cracks by the end of the twentieth century. The massification and commercialization of higher education made it hard for many teachers to engage in research, in turn creating a privileged stratum of researchers increasingly detached from teaching and catalyzing a mutual irritation between the civil sphere focusing on activism and many scholars stressing academic excellence and thus withdrawing from civic engagement. The Invisible University was also a response to this crisis of academia, experimenting, under the pressure of an unprecedented situation of mass dislocation of students and scholars, to relink the educational, research, and civic components in unconventional and innovative ways.

The fact that this project emerged in connection with Ukraine is not accidental. A deeper historical connection reaches back to the nineteenth century, linking education and civil society in contexts where the (imperial) state was considered "alien" and often directly inimical, and the educational and academic sphere could only be developed "below" or "above" the state, forming part of a "parallel polis." In the Russian Empire, Poles but also Ukrainians, Jews, and the Baltic nations developed such structures. Notably, the Nobel laureate physicist Maria Skłodowska-Curie and the Polish-Jewish educator and children's rights advocate Janusz Korczak emerged from these unofficial educational frameworks. This alternative modality also existed in the Western hemisphere in the form of institutions integrating refugee scholars, such as the New School for Social Research, and programs of workers' education: for instance, the Budapest-born economic sociologist Karl Polanyi developed his ideas on what became his famous book, *The Great Transformation* (1944), while lecturing at the Workers' Educational Association in Great Britain.

The history of the Ukrainian Underground University also matters in this context. Initiated in 1921 by Ukrainian student activists with an aim to resist the educational policies of the Polish government (that since 1919 controlled the province of Galicia), it gathered prominent Western Ukrainian academics, but its attempts to seek international recognition were futile. In an atmosphere of intensified nationalist violence on both sides, the university system, both official and underground, proved too vulnerable, and the underground university ceased to exist in 1925.

Underground (or "flying") universities emerged again in response to repressive political regimes in Eastern Europe in the second half of the twentieth century, especially within the dissident movements of the 1970s and 1980s. Key figures of CEU's founding generation were also linked to such projects, such as the Hungarian dissident Miklós Vásárhelyi, who first raised the idea of a Central European University; the critical historian of Central Europe, Péter Hanák, who served as the first history department chair at CEU; and the Oxford-based Canadian philosopher involved with the Prague flying university, William Newton-Smith, who became CEU's first executive chairperson. This tradition was also continued in the region in the 1990s in the form of invisible colleges that offered an intensive educational experience to motivated students, preparing them to act as catalysts of the region's modernization and democratization.

IUFU's institutional design drew on these traditions, reframed in light of the authoritarian backlash after 2010. This model was reinforced by the post-COVID technological innovations facilitating a hybrid mode of teaching. All this pointed toward a program of "hybrid education for hybrid regimes," focusing especially on scholars at risk—forced to emigrate or pushed out from the state educational system—as a resource.

Emergency Response and Reclaiming the Future

Ukraine was not a primary target of these concerns before February 2022. The war, starting in 2014 in Eastern Ukraine, dislocated many scholars and students, and the country had problems with corruption and power-grabbing, but it was not an authoritarian state in any way. The vibrant Ukrainian public sphere, revitalized after the Revolution of Dignity, was far from being dominated by a centralized government, as had happened in some Central European countries.

However, as the full-scale war started, Ukrainian higher education became gravely threatened: Russians shelled university buildings in many cities; many institutions had to suspend their regular operations; prominent scholars were killed by the occupiers on the streets of towns around Kyiv; many scholars and students were forced to leave their country; and others could only continue their studies in extremely challenging circumstances. Students and instructors in many Ukrainian universities started volunteering initiatives to help their army and fellow citizens, especially those fleeing from occupied or attacked territories. Some also volunteered to join the Armed Forces of Ukraine. The war divided time into "before" and "after" February 24, 2022, producing massive shock, grievance, and anger that rapidly devalued prewar habits, opinions, and views. Hence it was urgently important to reconnect in the academic space and to provide some sense of normality in these unthinkable circumstances.

While trying to support scholars we knew personally, we realized that the conventional support schemes targeting individual scholars at risk, usually providing short-term research scholarships in residence abroad, had few tangible benefits for students. With a group of CEU colleagues and affiliated scholars such as László Kontler, Renáta Uitz, and Vladimir Petrović, we started to think about how to reconnect students affected by the war with Ukrainian and international faculty. Oleksandr Shtokvych at the secretariat of the Open Society University Network (OSUN) provided invaluable support from the start. We also cooperated with the Ukrainian student group at CEU in Vienna that kept exerting pressure on the university administration to assist their Ukrainian peers at home.

Rather than following any kind of blueprint, IUFU emerged as an experiment in education and solidarity, developing new modalities and building dialogue across regional and national boundaries. It adjusts its institutional design to wartime challenges that otherwise make it hard for students to attend classes synchronically. Students earn European (ECTS) credits as part of CEU's non-degree program and then have them accredited at their respective institutions. From the very beginning, we were also aware of the limited impact of online classes and sought to create a possibility for face-to-face meetings. Consequently, we created the model of intensive summer and winter schools that now take place in both Budapest and Lviv, so that students who cannot cross the border may also participate.

As our main principle is to help as many students as possible, we also keep our organizational structure open to like-minded institutions and colleagues. Initially, the project was mainly based at the Budapest campus of CEU, with its primary support coming from OSUN. Since the fall semester of 2022, Imre Kertész Kolleg in Jena (Germany), under the directorship of Joachim von Puttkamer, has been our permanent partner, receiving support from the German Academic Exchange Service (DAAD). Gradually, other funding agencies such as the Porticus Foundation (The Netherlands), the John D. and Catherine T. MacArthur Foundation (US), the Institute of International Education (US), XTX Markets (UK), and the Mott Foundation (US) joined in with varying levels of financial support to fund individual courses, specific activities, or student stipends. All this made it possible to receive an ever-growing number of students, reaching more than 900 after the second year. What is more, our classes, online seminars, and summer and winter schools mobilized over 400 academic colleagues from Ukraine and across the world, acting as lecturers, language instructors, mentors, and directors in forty courses so far. To implement this program, we established partnerships with several universities and research institutions in Ukraine, including the Ivan Franko National University of Lviv, the Ukrainian Catholic University in Lviv, and Kyiv-Mohyla Academy in Kyiv, as well as the Lviv-based Center for Urban History of East Central Europe.

Most Ukrainian universities, even the ones based in cities that were directly affected by the war, were able to resume courses, at least in an online format, during the fall 2022 semester. Yet the interest in IUFU steadily increased. The educational space of IUFU engages students and scholars who are looking for new forms of academic solidarity and cooperation. The courses bring together students of different academic levels, from BA to PhD. From the interaction with the students who participated in the online courses and the first summer school, we understood that there was a demand for engaging in individual research and discussing it with peers and mentors. Gradually, this modality became another key component of IUFU, with around seventy students per semester implementing such projects on topics related to different cultural, political, historical, legal, or social questions faced by Ukrainian society at war. The aim of all these activities is to think together, developing and preserving a democratic political and academic culture while maintaining a pluralistic and open cultural space.

A Pedagogical Experiment

The educational structure of IUFU was designed very quickly after February 2022, partly because this model was rooted in the preexisting discussions and intellectual traditions mentioned above, but also because the war created urgency. The Ukrainian students and scholars who joined the initiative looked not only for an academic shelter but for a platform that allowed meaningful intellectual interaction, one where pressing concerns and questions could be articulated.

Most IUFU courses are directed by a duo or trio of scholars who represent both Ukrainian and non-Ukrainian academic cultures, and the individual classes are about bringing together different perspectives. This excludes "Westsplaining," instead seeking to intertwine regional, national, and global intellectual discourses. It also excludes national self-referentiality, or the idea that a culture can only be understood by insiders. Instead, we try to place questions relevant to Ukrainian students into a transnational comparative perspective. The English working language of the classes and thematic courses developed in cooperation with colleagues from former Yugoslavia, also integrating students from these countries, provided a framework for such a multiperspective and transnational approach. Our courses are thus different from regular university courses: they offer a platform on which Ukrainian and international scholars can reexamine their academic convictions from the perspective of the political, cultural, social, and moral reconfiguration brought forward by the war.

The unprecedented nature of the situation also upends the traditional logic of instruction, namely the transmission of a well-established "package" of knowledge from the teachers to the students. Emotionally and intellectually, the direction of transmission is often reversed: students' resilience and commitment inspire their teachers, and the reflections on the war bring up themes and sensitivities that are vanishingly rare in mainstream Western academia, not experiencing firsthand any war on their home territories since WWII.

IUFU is not just an educational project in the traditional sense. It is a constant dialogue and a radically democratic process of socialization. Transgressing the conventional logic of university instruction, we are experimenting with a variety of innovative formats. For instance, more advanced students participate in educating their junior peers. IUFU offers a possibility to reflect on the war as it is unfolding but also to think of it from the perspective of a possible post-war time when these students would become key actors in the reconstruction of the Ukrainian social and institutional texture. We sincerely hope that the students who will have gone through our program will make their voices heard on the future of Ukrainian higher education, and in a broader sense, on the political and cultural life of the country after the victorious peace we all hope for.

IUFU barely divides those who are organizing or teaching and those who are just "receiving." Everybody, including the professors, is a transmitter and receiver at the same time. In fact, from the very beginning, our program's crucial actors included PhD students and postdoctoral researchers from CEU and a wide range of Ukrainian, European, and American institutions. They acted as mentors facilitating intensive, intimate, small-group discussions. These meetings aired and clarified conceptual problems and contested issues raised in the online classes, themselves turning into ongoing research seminars where students could discuss their individual projects. The students, in turn, initiated their internet journal, *Visible Ukraine* (https://visibleukraine.org). Its objective is to amplify diverse Ukrainian voices, introduce new interdisciplinary subjects, and foster intellectual exchanges to make Ukraine visible in local, regional, and global discussions. Significantly, the lack of implicit hierarchy in the interaction was immediately striking: it was clear that students took the initiative. They were asking questions important to them, not being afraid to critically engage professors from Yale, Columbia, Princeton, Oxford, Paris, Amsterdam, or Berlin. These exchanges often generated exciting reactions among even more students as they became aware that there are no ready-made answers and that they must seek solutions in their own experiences.

IUFU also brings together different Ukrainian spatial and cultural perspectives. The Ukrainian community might seem homogeneous from the outside, but from the inside, it is complex and multilayered. There are considerable regional, linguistic, and religious divergences linked to multiple imperial legacies (Russian, Habsburg, Ottoman), the complex processes of industrialization, urbanization, population migrations, and the top-down identity-building policies of the Soviet period. Consequently, our classes permit diverse Ukrainian voices to represent different positions and forms of local knowledge, but at the same time, strive to create a common framework of critical reflection, interpretation, and acquaintance.

While rejecting a merely utilitarian approach to scholarly knowledge, the question of combating Russian propaganda, massively based on historical mythologies, remains relevant in the context of war. Over the last few years, the Ukrainian public discourse eagerly turned to the globally fashionable conceptual vocabulary of decolonization. However, it quickly became obvious that the framework of coloniality is more complex, and although it offers powerful intellectual and political tools, it also faces many challenges. For example, how to deconstruct the persistent Eurocentrism of the Ukrainian intellectual tradition while at the same time asserting to the outside world that Ukraine fights for common European democratic values.

Working toward a non-Russocentric understanding of the post-Soviet space remains a priority for IUFU. In this context, we also had to face the dilemma of how to engage with knowledge production in Russia and by Russians, a question also posed by many other transnational initiatives working with scholars at risk. As we stated on our website at the very beginning, we categorically excluded cooperation with scholars retaining any affiliation with any Russian state institution or anyone remaining silent about the Russian aggression. At the same time, a number of Russian colleagues who protested the invasion and emigrated after being targeted by the authorities for their critical stance (some of them also making efforts to rethink their research in a "decolonial" framework), were invited to contribute by coteaching some of the individual classes. Ironically, but not unexpectedly, our statement was read as "anti-Russian" by the Russian Prosecutor General's office, justifying its decision to designate CEU an "undesirable organization" in October 2023.

IUFU reacts to what is going on in the present, but it also seeks to catalyze debates on the future. In this sense, IUFU is also meant as a pilot project for similar hybrid initiatives targeting societies where academic freedom is threatened or undermined. Along these lines, we have organized joint seminars with scholars at risk from Turkey, Belarus, Serbia, Hungary, Nicaragua, Brazil, and other countries. Just as our networks united to donate power banks that allowed our students to run their computers and classes despite black-outs, we now aim to gather resources, ideas, and inspiration to strengthen the democratic resilience of Ukrainian society and any who look to this example, eager to charge the power banks of democracy.

Democratic Engagement in Wartime

Power banks can be considered symbols of Ukrainians' resilience during this war, storing energy for moments of emergency and thus making it possible to maintain some normality. Pursuing this metaphor further implies that it is not enough to focus on saving capacities for the postwar time, as many projects tended to formulate their principal task in the initial phase of the war. Democratic practices cannot be merely suspended and relegated to the postwar period. There is an obvious need to engage politically even during wartime, both in terms of controlling the different branches of power and articulating possible visions of the future that society can internalize and pursue. We organized our last IUFU Winter School in January 2024 along these lines, focusing on the cultural, political, ethical, legal, and philosophical implications of the prolonged state of emergency. We discussed with Ukrainian and international experts how warfare can coexist with democratic institutions and how it is possible to exercise democratic rights and even protest specific policies while being responsible for the survival of the political community and its institutions.

Rather than giving definitive answers, these discussions made it clear that the paradigms commonly used to navigate these problems in Western academia (often predicated upon an internal type of violence rather than a full-scale war) are inadequate to describe the current Ukrainian situation. There is a pressing need to rethink the war experience, reflecting on its changing temporality. From this discussion, other questions followed: about the distribution of the burdens of the war, the internal dynamic of the Ukrainian public sphere, the tension between the imperative of national unity and the plurality of positions and opinions, and the possibility of political dissent and action in wartime.

These dilemmas brought together a group of IUFU students into an essay-writing seminar led by Tetiana Zemliakova, who also designed the 2024 Winter and Summer School programs, and Guillaume Lancereau. It aimed to engage with the major issues Ukrainian society is facing from the perspective of the students who began their university studies not much before the Russian invasion, and who were hit by the experience of the full-scale war precisely when they started to formulate their academic interests. In this sense, it became impossible to separate the scholarly and existential dimensions of their engagement. Hence, the seminar sought to transcend the opposition between the two common approaches to the war: on the one hand, the detached, purely academic papers, and on the other, the emotional firsthand comments on dramatic and often tragic developments. What we sought instead to achieve is the reassessment of war as a fundamental state of existence.

We asked the students to start from their own experiences and go beyond them, reflecting on how the past two years of war have altered established intellectual categories, procedures, and modes of political engagement. As the situation is unprecedented, there are no guidelines to follow. Thus, all contributors had to find their way to a chosen theme by formulating new questions and, in some cases, developing a new conceptual language and new authorial positions to express their ideas. The results of these intensive group discussions are this collection of short essays in the original sense of the word: open-ended attempts to grasp, define, understand, or problematize certain phenomena, inviting the reader, who is most likely not in a war situation, to think and feel together with us.

We are pleased to present these essays by students of the Invisible University and by some of our most committed mentors, without whose work the pedagogical process of IUFU would be unimaginable. While some of these mentors are not Ukrainians, the war also affected them on many levels (existentially, politically, professionally) as they experienced it through their civic engagements and work at IUFU, spending long hours every week with their mentees.

The texts are loosely organized in three thematic clusters, but due to the nature of their development, they speak to each other beyond the confines of these sections. The clusters disclose three specific features of democratic action in wartime in general, and of the Ukrainian predicament in particular. The first cluster, "Front Lines," features the self-reflective observations of young Ukrainian intellectuals on the multiple threats of war, both physical and mental. The principal front line involves Ukrainian academics fighting for the political, intellectual, and cultural survival of their country—both directly (as soldiers and civil volunteers) and indirectly (as educators and voices in the public sphere). The war situation dramatically raises the stakes of intellectual and societal engagement while highlighting the importance of open and critical reaction to external threats and internal cleavages.

Ukrainian society reacted swiftly and effectively to the full-scale invasion because of its preexisting war experience dating to 2014 and the highly developed and differentiated civil sphere, providing know-how and human resources for social and military mobilization. The tacit democratic "social contract" emerging between the government and the population after the Russian attack generated intense voluntary participation in the war effort, both at the front and in the hinterland. This contract also entailed the self-limiting behavior of the state in terms of respecting many democratic rights (including relative freedom of the press, movement, and political criticism) even under martial law. However, as this contract was primarily based on unspoken rules, it could hardly serve as a basis of negotiation between the government and many social groups. With the prolongation of the war, the depletion of human resources, and the increasing politicization of differences between the war experiences of those who stayed in the country and those who remained abroad or left after February 2022, the debate over the sense of just distribution of the war burden has intensified. This ongoing debate touches upon the relationship between, on the one hand, those who volunteered for the army or were immediately mobilized and their families, and on the other hand, those who were spared from mobilization (including university students, researchers, and instructors). Other differences arise between those living in the country and the refugees abroad, those internally displaced from the East and those living in the relatively safer Western zones, Ukrainian versus Russian speakers, and more.

Seeking to exercise the faculty of judgment, our texts reflect on the ways a democratic political culture can engage with such divergences and cleavages, sustaining plurality but at the same time maintaining a common political framework necessary for the war effort. However, preserving the political framework to mediate between different interests is not enough to sustain a democratic polity in times of war. Necessary, too, is conscious democratic action by different groups and individuals who seek new ways to cooperate internally and externally.

Consequently, the second cluster of essays, "Solidarity," ponders the different modalities of cooperation and its normative and affective preconditions. Far from being predicated exclusively on national belonging, the call for solidarity is crucial for Ukrainians seeking to urge the external world to help the Ukrainian state and individual citizens affected by the war. In turn, solidarity is also a central modality for non-Ukrainians to engage with the war, offering logistical, economic, or academic help. The changing parameters of international assistance over time, with the shifting focus of world politics, pose severe challenges to any efficient action of self-defense. Solidarity is thus not a given but a result of continuous dialogue. Hence, it remains central to democratic practice and theory as an imperative of joint action, an affective basis for a productive exchange of opinions, and as a possible result of sincere political and cultural debate during wartime.

Wars have their temporality, and people have their ways of coping with the changing realities of war. The third section, "Endurance," engages with this dynamic. The military situation fluctuates constantly, and so do the community's horizons of expectation. In the beginning, no one was sure about what would happen the very next day, but there was a widespread consensus about the ending of the war within a short timeframe. Later, the direct war experience became routinized, and people became more confident of what the next day might bring. However, they also became much less confident about the proximity of a definitive ending. While the individual experiences of war are naturally divergent, their accumulation feeds into institutional practices as well as individual and group behavior. The traumatic experience of violence cuts into the fabric of society, making it especially hard to sustain the conventional channels of deliberation. Hence, a key precondition of democratic action in war is the ability to cope with the unexpected and retain the capacity for self-reflection even in moments of extreme hardship. While wars are waged by collectivities, the task of self-reflection cannot be delegated to institutions or social groups but remains an individual responsibility.

By seeking to mediate these different experiences in the face of a constant threat of death, a democratic community at war is testing the very limits of democratic theory and practice, offering a unique vantage point for those who are not at war. To facilitate this process, the contributions to this volume present the plurality of voices in a transnational democratic community, bringing together Ukrainian students and scholars with their international peers, sharing and reflecting on the transformative experience of learning from each other in a situation when all participants are confronted by fundamental questions about their ethical commitments, agency, life, and vision of the future.

Part I

Front Lines

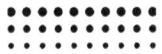

1

The Urgency to Live

LIANA BLIKHARSKA

I encountered this man in a museum. That place has recently become the repository of decommunized monuments whose significance is measured by their bygone symbolism or their creators' names. "I saw them dismantling it," the man said as I passed him. He looked at the two parts of the Glory Monument, which once stood on Stryiska Street in Lviv. Now, these two colossal bronze figures—the Motherland and the Red Army soldier stripped of their roles as sites of pilgrimage, ceremony, and reverence—lay atop several pallets before us. "There were many people; they quickly toppled it down with a crane and loaded it in the truck. It was a lovely day, and I'm happy they demolished it. Right in time."

In time is an intriguing phrase, one I hear all too frequently lately. "It's time to unite and become a cohesive force," "Discussing trauma and memory is just in time," "The time came to write a book about war," "Now is the apt time to live and celebrate life," and so on. There are so many disparate things that Ukrainian society labels as opportune in this way. Does anyone have a pen? I need to make a brief remark in the margins: these "timely" expressions have nothing to do with time. They simply veil the inner sense of righteousness that suddenly becomes apparent to everyone, awaiting an antiphon to begin the service. But who is to sing?

War exists on its own terms and according to its own time; it is about speed and urgency. The sense of urgency overwhelms and demands immediate action. "You have to act, if you want to survive"—I cannot recall where I encountered this motto. I might have conceived of it myself when hearing the air-raid sirens for the first time. When the sirens go off, we have ten to fifteen minutes to seek shelter. War does not tolerate slowness. Nonetheless, you become accustomed to being late for a half-second, always late. "It should have been done yesterday," people say. The feeling of a very slight delay is omnipresent.

In peaceful times, people usually imagine tomorrow and rarely doubt its arrival. In war, our morale reverses. Everything pivotal should be done today because tomorrow might never come, and the urgency begins here. Someone weaves a camouflage net or dispatches aid to the soldiers while they are still breathing; another hurries to topple statues and thus secure their town from the contested past; yet another pleads on their socials to close the skies over Ukraine now. Not everything that people do necessarily brings a decisive advantage to the country. What is sure, however, is that these actions are made in war and out of the war's urgency.

After the war, when they ask you, "What were you doing?" how will you respond? And what if you ask this question of yourself? Society, in its quest for survival and salvation of its soul, urges you to answer. Society will not pardon your passivity on the Day of Reckoning. How do I ensure that I am doing enough when people kill and are being killed? I tell myself, "I'm not on the front line, so I must do something helpful anywhere I am; I must work for victory." In 2022, old words were resurrected when civilians began talking again about cultural, economic, and even family fronts. Being helpful means having at your disposal another day when you can act again. "If you're not on the front lines, not killing enemies, then you must justify your existence in the rear"—these phrases sounded through Ukrainian society most sharply at the beginning of the war, both in 2014 and 2022. A permanent feeling of urgency haunts everyone and drags us down. And no matter its strength, it is easy to substitute fear, guilt, or even courage in its place. The internal pleas and external calls accord into a single imperative for action whose sources remain obscure.

To discriminate between singular voices in the chorus of urgency, one requires something that war does not afford—an extra minute of thinking. People in war believe they can survive by acting, but how can one decide which action to take? In times of peace, the urgency is born from life itself and powers continuous thought and action. In wartime, the urgency is born from death; you act to delay death by at least a half-second more. Whose death? Death is no longer limited to one's own body but is extended to everyone: it is now projected onto our shared future. And the fear of death now means the fear of what would come after it, because all of us will be judged, whether we survive or die fighting. Actions in war should be taken quickly and decisively. Even if some actions appear unnecessary and their significance to the war effort is questionable; a survivor can still say: "We were at war, and everyone did something, and so did I, for I just wanted to remain alive."

In war, every action is thought to be ultimate, and what was an ongoing process now might be the last convulsion of a living being. Does it matter if we organize another exhibition in Western galleries when thousands of artworks were turned to ashes in the last few years? What difference does it make when we rename another city that was leveled to the ground, and write a volume on democratic resilience? Adding the qualifier "urgent" to any action makes it easier to perform, for it exempts us from judgment and responsibility—urgency allows us to turn away death for another half-second. We say "in time" to enchant death and grasp another moment to make sure that we are still alive.

2

Target(ed) Audiences

KATERYNA OSYPCHUK

Watching the war from afar means looking at a photo montage. This distant observation deprives images of depth and dimension, flattening them to their surface. What remains are the displaced, unrelatable cutouts. This cramped heterogeneity of the digital media space connects war with everyday life, yet never merges the two for a distant observer. I am not a distant observer. For me, the presence of war in the media is not the rupture of the surface but the excess of signs. I open the newsfeed and get dizzy because of this superimposition: someone's vacation photos, the footage of my hometown damaged by Russian missiles, a eulogy for someone younger than me, and a birthday fundraiser for drones. Being inside, I see the war duplicating itself in the media, transgressing its borders, and becoming nonlocalizable. Watching the war from afar instead implies mediation, which reproduces the distance. This distance protects—the social media algorithms limit exposure to "sensitive images" for the ones observing afar. To watch the war from afar is, thus, to be stuck in the surface's precarity, in photographs' inability to reveal anything but the indexical, the digital traces of physical pain. And even that, from a distance, too often remains unseen.

To show the war from the inside is to issue too many invitations. It means trying to turn all the media inside out to bring the observer closer and to invent a new language for bridging the abysses between seeing and understanding. It is to invite one to our understandings. I share war photographs because I feel isolated in violence. I share the "cruel images,"[4] spilling the pain that I carry, and the media kindly offers me more: "You might be interested in …" Showing the war from the inside means trying to share the lenses from your own retinas. It means speaking visually, exposing one's suffering in hopes of being heard, understood, and relieved.

The Russo–Ukrainian war is supposedly the "most documented conflict in history," considering the amount and variety of visual means used in articulating it. This (over) production of images, ranging from photographs taken by journalists to footage from drones and combatants' cameras, enables others to access the war zones unseen otherwise. Since February 2022, the attitude toward these photographs has changed along with their purpose. Initially, sharing war footage was prohibited because of the danger of disclosing military secrets. Later, the images were instrumentalized to garner support—mainly the images of destruction. These photographic documents serve both "internal" and "external" audiences. Bracketing the war into separate frames, the images distance it from the diverging witnesses, helping the internal audience to cope with the changing reality and allowing the external audience to understand and react to it. Being shared with calls for action, these photographs seem to participate in the symbolic exchange of gaining support in return for revealing the vulnerability of the wartime conditions. In this communicative situation, the medium complicates the actors' engagement. It doubles the roles of the "sufferers" by turning them into witnesses and then, by constructing the images of the depicted and the observers, it enforces the divides between "we" who suffer and "they" who observe, between "we," the spectators, and the suffering "them."

For many Ukrainians, seeing "cruel images" is inseparable from redistributing them. Here, seeing is transformed into the labor of witnessing, and the ones who face the war-torn "reality" come forward to share it. Thus, the role of photographs has changed from an index to a gesture. Reposting the images of the Russian attacks became a form of involvement in warfare that brings documentation in enunciating the emergency. The depictions of the suffering "self" are paradoxically used for mobilizing the "other." This form of visual rhetoric asks for an immediate reaction, implying that the internal and external audiences share the same relationship with the photographs' referents.

The images constitute a form of rhetoric that promises no metaphorical distance. They point to their subjects and render them visible, demonstrating the unspeakable, substituting the verbal in articulating the rupture—a medium straightforward enough because of its "rawness." However, an image is never only an index. Even the documentary photograph employs an "image scenario," a framework we use to make sense of the changing reality. These ultra-familiar frames connect ongoing events with existing knowledge, bringing them closer and making them more understandable.[5] This representation mode imposes old interpretative procedures onto current events, which distances viewers from the emergency. The most documented war is the most mediated and, thereby, the most distanced one as well.

In the Ukrainian context, visual articulation is accompanied by verbal. This form of speech is concentrated in bits: #russiaisaterroriststate, #closethesky, #armUkraine, as if the short form of the messages could help them reach farther and faster. Ironically, these were the images I saw on my newsfeed as if I were their target audience, the one who needed an explanation and motivation to act.

If the images constitute a form of rhetoric, whose gaze do we follow, and who do we look at? Articulating the unfolding events, Ukrainian users employ individual stories to express a collective affect. Sharing "cruel images," we speak on behalf of and through the affected ones of "ours." Yet, the witnesses stay silent themselves, remaining a projection of a collective self, iconic in speeches of others. After the deoccupation of the Kyiv region, Ukrainian users started a flash mob to show the crimes the Russian army committed there. The picture of a participant was followed by an image of a person killed and the following text: "This is my photo on the left. But this could also have been my photo on the right. Each of us could be killed by the Russians because we are Ukrainians." The selfies posted along with the photographs of the tortured and killed, as well as the "it could have been me" phrases, illustrated not only the ultimate absence of a safe place in Ukraine but also the rediscovery of collective belonging. This is the only closeness these images foster—the one embodying targeted audiences' "other-ache."[6] It is almost like saying, "I am alive, and I bear no physical pain myself, yet I carry the pain of the ones I identify with." It could have been me because I am Ukrainian too, and our shared identity is the reason we are under threat. The community is reimagined through witnessing, which is simultaneously embodied and mediated.

The sight is shaped by a situation, and the conditions of seeing an image inform its status and functions. The photographs of the "most documented war" are watched online. This "digital witnessing" unfolds at the nexus of technology and isolation, each mutually enhancing the other. Providing audiences with the materials they express interest in, the mediascape appears to have a well-defined place for everyone it encompasses: this is "we" who share the images, and "us" who are faced with them; these are the tags we use to raise awareness around the world—the tags that one cannot find from non-Ukrainian IP addresses.[7]

This "digital witnessing" is also informed by the convergence of the restrictions on war-related content and overexposure to images. Social media platforms label the depictions of the Russian attacks' aftermath as "sensitive" and hide them from view; more so, they introduce the option to "limit the political content." With such restrictions in place, it is even easier to turn away from the war in a mediascape designed for entertainment, and the algorithms already do that for distant observers. At the same time, the iconomanic character of the media space and overexposure to violence also inform the process of witnessing, turning what remains seen into a two-dimensional spectacle.

On February 16, 2022, eight days before Russia invaded Ukraine for the second time, Reuters started a live stream from Kyiv. A few days before, the US had issued a warning about the possibility of a Russian attack in the following days. The agency aimed to document it immediately in the heart of the Ukrainian capital, in high resolution and real-time, making the stream available worldwide. This attempt at documentation made me feel lost in a spectacle I did not consent to participating in.

The genre of documentary presupposes the utopia of a controlled witnessing, of having the chance to follow unfolding events from a safe place far away. Photography enables this form of witnessing by converging human and machine gazes, constructing the sight that presents itself as unmediated, raw, and objective. Yet, accelerating to the automatized footage, losing its author, and being shared en masse, photography risks failing its "civil contract." Circulated in the mediascape that flattens the represented mediums onto seemingly similar surfaces and limits interaction with them, the photographic gesture gets stuck in the media-produced isolation and points at itself.

War photographs mobilize the community sharing them by referring to the collective belonging and the sense of threat it entails in wartime. Sharing these images in a mediascape that conceals the distances it is built upon implies the perception of them as a shared dispositif, hence of having the same actuality.[8] Approaching photography as the most direct and objective medium, "we" expect a similar reaction from "them," forgetting that understanding the images depends on the conditions of seeing. This ensuing short-sightedness—of the ones seeing nothing but war and others having a limited chance to witness it from a distance—can be explained by the specificities of the visual articulation in the wartime mediascape. The images intended to evoke understanding and mobilize "others" have diverging relations between their referents and audiences. As they are shared on social media, they seem only to deepen the distance between the ones depicted and the ones who observe.

3

Scholars at Risk?

OLEKSII RUDENKO

The incomplete list of Ukrainian scholars and students killed by Russia since the beginning of the aggression in 2014 would be longer than the graduation list of most universities. If one limits the enumeration to historians killed in action only in 2024, it would include Maksym Shtatskyi, a researcher of the history of Mennonites (aged thirty-five), who fought in the 79th Airborne Assault Brigade. It would include Serhiy Rybak, National University of Kyiv-Mohyla Academy history graduate and father of three (aged forty-seven). It would also include Viacheslav Zalevskyi, a historian-reconstructor and volunteer of the Vinnytsia History Center, who was killed at the age of twenty-four while serving as a soldier of the 12th Special Operation Brigade "Azov." While numerous scholars joined the Ukrainian Armed Forces, many others accepted diverse research positions that opened in Western universities to advance Ukrainian scholarship.

Western academia responded to the beginning of the full-scale Russian war against Ukraine by launching numerous emergency research programs, scholarships, and grants for endangered Ukrainian students and faculty—and we are grateful for them. Within this framework, however, dozens of baffling announcements appeared. For instance, one of them stated, "We offer our support to Ukrainian, Russian, and international students who had their education compromised." Another institution advertised scholarships for students from Ukraine, Russia, and Belarus "who are experiencing financial difficulties due to the current situation." There were also postgraduate scholarships for displaced students from the same three countries, and another program offered "equal opportunities to researchers of Ukrainian or Russian nationality." Some of these programs reframed earlier initiatives to integrate Ukrainians; others were designated for Ukrainians in early spring 2022 and later extended to include Belarusians and Russians, and some equated the three nationalities from the very beginning.

What these announcements have in common is their ability to provoke emotions varying from surprise to outrage among Ukrainian scholars who are considering applying for them. Those who lost their academic networks and opportunities as a direct result of aggression find themselves equated with those related to the aggression directly or indirectly. At least, such is the wording. Numerous "scholars at risk" descriptions treat Ukrainian and Russian academics under the unifying label, "affected by war." Whether the tendency to equate hardships arises from ignorance or insensitivity, it remains undoubtedly dangerous because it intentionally overlooks the fact of Russian aggression against Ukraine. No clear distinction is made, and while the institution may publicly support Ukraine's defense, such a framing makes many doubt the institution's sincerity and forethought. Is it ready to accept Ukrainian students and researchers who suffer from PTSD after witnessing genocidal war and continuous aerial bombardments? Or is it just as interested in providing additional office desks for Russian scholars who emigrated for any other reason besides the complete destruction of their cities?

The academic world presents itself as a space open for debate and discussion that can accommodate a broad spectrum of opinions. Hence, the community's members are expected to share fundamental values such as respect, equality, and freedom of speech. The least prominent but not least important aspect of maintaining this world is the sense of academic solidarity toward those in need or danger, which has been a driving force behind numerous offerings addressing Ukrainian, Russian, and sometimes Belarusian scholars and students since the spring of 2022. Nonetheless, what appears as benevolence in times of peace translates into hypocrisy in times of war. The Ukrainian academic community is fighting for its survival, and its "emergency" is unquestionable: research institutions and universities are destroyed across the country from Kharkiv to Lviv, including the Boychuk Art Academy and the Kharkiv National University of Economics; archives, museums, and libraries are either evacuated or burned down; and any work is constantly interrupted by air-raid sirens, missiles, and drone strikes. In the case of those representing Russian academia, "emergencies" vary from discomfort to fear of retaliation for various levels of dissent.

Wording matters. Every "and" put between Ukrainian and Russian scholars tacitly victimizes them in the same manner. Similar is the effect of vague formulas like "displaced scholars" that blur distinctions between scholars' backgrounds exactly where those should be clarified. For people under attack, lumping these hardships together appears obnoxious, for they know all too well who the aggressor responsible for this war is. Yet, Ukrainian scholars need to apply to continue their academic careers and get funding that will help them survive for at least some time. Meanwhile, academia wants to look ostensibly equitable and thus loses sight of solidarity and justice. While publicly condemning Russian war crimes and military aggression, it attempts to take a middle ground, which undermines its intentions of restoring justice toward victims.

My most recent participation in a large international conference was the ASEEES Convention in November 2022. The State Border Service did not grant me permission to leave Ukraine, so my colleagues took over the panel I had assembled and organized. They kindly assisted me in presenting my paper via Zoom, although the conference rules prohibited it. Furthermore, because Russia started striking Ukrainian power plants, my presentation was interrupted by blackouts. I am curious to know how things are at other academic events abroad, given that Russian scholars, especially those already abroad, may join them with much fewer hurdles than Ukrainian ones, especially men who may not obtain permission to leave the country under martial law. One may argue that it was the Ukrainian government that closed the state borders for some categories of men, so it is the entity to blame. But would it have ever happened without the Russian invasion? The aggressor is responsible for my missed ASEEES conference, not the Ukrainian Border Service. I wish I could pursue one of many research opportunities in my field that have appeared since 2022. Instead, I am now exploring slightly different fields in Ukraine.

Ukrainian scholarship cannot equitably use the Western resources that have become available since the war: only those who have left and joined Western structures may access them. Hence, academic solidarity becomes paradoxically selective and biased against scholars who switched from their smart-casual to military-casual style. Many Ukrainian scholars prioritized their volunteering, service, and fighting for their families and country over methodology and publications in top-ranked journals because their survival is at stake. Is the same true for Russian scholars? Very few articulate their opposition to the Russian war; even many émigrés remain conspicuously silent. The majority, however, hope that the war will end soon, and they will resume being a part of the international community as if Russia never attacked Ukraine and the war never happened. However, the war goes on.

Among other things, Western academia claims to be founded on equal access, merit, and fair competition. In other words, the best application gets funding, and the best candidate gets promoted in the academic job market. However, many Ukrainians have little opportunity to prepare their applications (*memento* blackouts) or struggle to collect documents in wartime chaos. Meanwhile, Russian scholars can freely apply, and thanks to vague formulations such as "affected by war," they are the ones to get the offers. The allegedly liberal Russian scholars thus receive an opportunity to promote Russian narratives while Ukrainian voices get lost. Although the Russo–Ukrainian war awakened interest in Eastern European studies and critical studies in Russian colonialism, the field remains filled mainly by scholars socialized in Russian academia whose perspective is not unbiased. At the same time, non-Russocentric scholarship remains underfunded. Additionally, hosting seemingly anti-Putin scholars carries the risk of infiltration: as ruled by an Estonian Court, the international relations scholar Professor Viacheslav Morozov from the University of Tartu combined his academic work with espionage for Russia.

Ukrainian scholars are not the only ones facing the calamity of destructive war. Therefore, it is even more important to consider measures of positive discrimination, a just attitude, and the trauma affecting most of the Ukrainian scholars, which should also be mirrored in the grant and scholarship schemes for those "at risk." What is just is not always equal. In the case of sensitive topics—and what can be more sensitive than the ongoing war that has affected *all* Ukrainian scholars?—a definite stand on a seemingly minor issue of wording would be appreciated by Ukrainian scholars as much as by any observer with an acute sense of equity.

4

Crimes in the Crime

SASHA KOKHAN

The full-scale Russian invasion of Ukraine caught me in Irpin. I stayed there for ten days and left before the city was occupied completely. On the fifth day, I went to buy some bread and saw two men staggering around and looking as if they had no clue where to go. They could have been either Russian saboteurs or random drug addicts; any explanation felt plausible. These were ten days of war, yet was it a siege, an occupation, or something else? One thing was certain: no part of the war happened the way I had imagined a war might look.

On February 24, 2022, the world collapsed and stopped making sense, but it persisted. I had to refigure what was plausible, what was dangerous, and what was necessary, but I did not know how to do it. Beginning with plausibility, I started reading media, mostly Telegram channels. As I read about the missile hits and scrolled the photo feed, Telegram began replacing my eyes and interpreting what my ears heard: after a loud bang, I checked the feed and expected it to explain what was happening. I turned to YouTube, news outlets, and blogs a few months later, assuming they knew something that would make this war understandable. So, I learned numerous arguments that converged on a single logic: there were Russians who launched missiles and did so to kill Ukrainians and destroy the Ukrainian state. Each medium seemed to make sense of something in its own way, but how? There were raw facts, grandiose interpretations, and facts combined with interpretations that disagreed with one another and, most important, with my own experience.

Strictly speaking, relying on experience would imply that the only verifiable knowledge of this war comes from what I touch with my own hands and see with my own eyes. During those ten days in Irpin, there was little coherence between what I could experience and what I could explain; sometimes there was no coherence at all. I heard missiles hitting the buildings every other minute but never saw them. Once, I saw some rising smoke, and another time, a piece of a military aircraft in my neighbor's yard. And were I even more exposed to the immediate experience of war, would it help me better understand that February 24 happened and continued? I witnessed the crime of war and witnessed war crimes, but I still cannot make sense of them.

The full-scale Russian invasion of Ukraine is a crime against humanity. This horrific crime of war allows for numerous concrete war crimes to be committed by particular humans. Often, these two definite instances are hard to distinguish from each other; furthermore, the media discourse explains them through each other. I read an interview with a Ukrainian philosopher who claimed that "Russians are a historical disease," and he continued by stating that any person who says, "I am Russian," at the same time says, "I am an imperialist, I am a xenophobe, I hate humanity." What is proposed is a single explanation of the war and its horrors based on nationhood. "The Russian" at once refers to one who commits the crime of war and the one who commits the war crimes.

There are crimes committed by Russians, indeed, by specific humans. And yet, how can we explain all the miseries and horrors that were not caused directly by Russian artillery—elderly people dying of heart attacks after hearing a nearby explosion or animals drowning after the destruction of the Kakhovka Dam? I flounder in my attempts to establish causal links and evaluate those responsibilities. However, it seems indispensable to make sense of the world I live in. I saw losses and destruction. But what if I had encountered Russian spies or saboteurs who infiltrated Irpin during those ten days, dressed as civilians in order to snoop? I might have; I don't know. I imagine having a dialogue with a war criminal who is Russian and whose motivation to commit a crime is precisely the one circulating in Ukrainian media, yet I doubt that this dialogue would make things more meaningful. Asking war criminals about their motives would likely achieve nothing, and at best would only help explain particular war crimes, yet at this level, there is no way to explain the crime of war.

Returning to the media, I read that "for over 300 years, Ukraine and Moscow have been in a permanent war for survival." Although somewhat varying, these metahistorical narratives tell us about the eternal struggle between "them," Russians, who have always been aggressors, and "us," Ukrainians, who have always been either suffering from "them" or resisting "them." Moreover, as experts say, we knew it all along. This interpretation roots the war in national frictions between Ukraine and Russia and presents it as an episode of an infinite happening. There was always war, there is war, and the war will forever continue. For me, only making sense of my world matters. And thus, I ask: If the war is eternal, what happened on February 24?

Media might explain the specifics of particular war crimes, but these specifics do not explain the crime of war. Using nationality as an explanatory factor is a compromise to the unexplainable—someone's readiness to threaten the life of others. Although Telegram was helpful initially, later I listened to historians and philosophers who seemed to understand; I also examined my memory because it is a witness's memory, and still I struggle to make sense of my ten days in Irpin. Maybe the frustration is that I conflated two crimes and sought one explanation for them both, or maybe that I failed to merge my personal experience with the information appearing on my phone screen. Experts might explain particular war crimes, but ultimately, the crime of war repels explanation, repels understanding, repels *knowing*. Indeed, I will be clueless again if I live long enough to witness another war.

5

The Side Effects of War

DENYS TERESHCHENKO

In the spring of 2023, a friend confided in me that she was distraught over some Ukrainian men who were unwilling to fight in the army and sought ways to not get mobilized; some of her friends had already enlisted voluntarily. I understood her reasons for thinking this way, although musing over other people's lives and wishing that they would go to war seemed frivolous to me. After all, while others' bodily integrity and lives were at stake, hers remained untouched. I personally cannot be angry with those who have not joined the ranks. I would first have to expect the same of myself, even if the law exempts me from being drafted for now.

Immediately after the invasion, many people enlisted because they felt a sense of duty, believing that the war would quickly come to an end. I did not have illusions that this would be the case. Later, after the success of the Kharkiv and Kherson offensives, we were told by the government and media that some new miraculous advance—the much-promised *kontrnastup*—would help to improve Ukraine's position remarkably. Some believed it, decided to join the army, and were bitterly disillusioned. The Western weapons that Ukraine was promised for this advance eventually came but were too scarce and arrived too late. By that time, the Russian forces had already built their defenses.

Today, nobody is even promising us an end to the war. We are stuck in this war; this war is stuck to us against our will; we are in it for the long haul. Too much has been bet by all sides in this increasingly fractured world. Meanwhile, attrition has sapped our ranks, and the military keeps repeating that it needs more people. After months of debates, the parliament passed a new law on mobilization, introducing harsher measures intended to replenish the army. One of my university peers was mobilized compulsorily, almost by accident, when he went to the draft board to update his data. He expected to receive a temporary, work-related exemption. Another friend, on the other hand, volunteered preemptively so that he could choose a military unit of his liking, worried that he might otherwise end up in an assault brigade.

The risk of paying for the country's defense with your own life becomes surer the longer you are in the army. What would I be ready to die for? The motivations of those who fight vary. My father's friend, a laborer from Poltava, voluntarily enlisted in the army together with my dad in the first days of the invasion; he said that he went to war "not for

Ukraine but so that the Buryats do not fuck my wife." A former university classmate from Lviv, a prominent activist, volunteer, and Ukrainian patriot, joined the Forces of Defense long before the invasion. Her posthumous letter said that she eventually felt free for the first time in her life after the big war started. "I want all of us to fight. As long as needed." She died in late spring 2024. My friend's ex, an anthropologist and leftist activist, volunteered to serve in the army because he felt an inner duty to protect his relatives and friends. After his first combat missions, he had trouble coming to terms with the realization that he had killed. A few months later, a shell explosion killed him.

I do not believe in the afterlife. When my friends, relatives, and I die, we will no longer exist. I have neither a wife to protect nor property to defend, although there are people in Ukraine whom I love and care for. I do not feel contented that this war helps mold Ukrainians' sense of national self, and even if it does, the price is too high. However, many other, much poorer men in smaller towns and villages are required by law and the authorities to put their bodies at the disposal of other people for an indefinite number of years and even risk their lives. It is a unique mobilization: nobody, for more than half a century in any European country, has asked so much from so many people who have been given so little.

The Ukrainian government knows its voters and reasonably fears losing popularity because of the ongoing mobilization. Hence, it implements the law carefully, step by step, despite the military's growing demands. The parliamentary opposition does not miss any opportunity to criticize the government, whatever moves it takes, and the mobilization effort appears simultaneously as "too little" for some and "too much" for others. Some voices, pro-Russian politicians and bloggers, mostly from abroad, insist on immediate negotiations instead. Meanwhile, the militant radicals, outside of and within the army, are resentfully observing the government's leniency and are appalled by the almost treacherous sluggishness of their compatriots. In their confrontation with both the "passive" compatriots and the government, they dig in and double down on calling for total mobilization, threatening the public that "everybody will fight." They insist on the fairer redistribution of death and call for a draft of those not yet affected by the war, specifically the ones in cities and abroad. Thus emerges an artificial dichotomy between the militant radicals, who went through the catharsis of war and want the whole country to follow them, and the short-sighted peace doves in Ukraine and Europe, who knowingly or unknowingly suggest solutions that would let the predator have his lunch.

Yet the enemy is real, and men and women on the front lines need help. Many could still be alive if reinforcements had come on time and in sufficient numbers; many more could take a pause and rest for a while, avoiding exhaustion. But should they, or the newly recruited, offer their bodies and lives unconditionally to merely preserve the *status quo ante bellum*? Although many agree that we should stop Russia, I do not see anyone in Ukraine, Europe, or the US who is both able and willing to ensure that this war can genuinely end in a stable peace without Russia's recidivist attack or the prospect of a Bosnian-like postwar destitution. Neither the US nor the European Union seems ready to guarantee our security after the ceasefire as the US did in, say, South Korea. Neither is prepared to fund Ukraine's infrastructure unconditionally and not for mere profit.

It is the sobering absurdity of death in this war, and perhaps in any war, that stands out to me. Why would anyone wage a war intending for it to never end? This absurdity begets all kinds of interpretations, and people are struggling to come up with explanations not only for one's own possible death but also of the deaths of others. Reasons for death are sometimes invented retrospectively: for Ukraine, the family, or freedom. Some say Ukrainians are defending the free world. This is the same free world that in its majority does not know it is being defended, and even when it does, it barely imagines the price and thus hesitates to pay its share for the service provided. Perhaps an honest reaction to the deaths of others precludes its rationalization altogether. I can only explain my own death.

I recall a conversation with my father as he was recovering from a wound received when his unit retreated from Soledar. In the hospital, he met a group of men of my age from the Bukovinian countryside. Unlike my father, they claimed, they were mobilized forcibly, regardless of whether they were sick, healthy, or exempted from service. They, however, did not desert and were sent for medical treatment after being wounded in combat. "Don't you dare go back to Ukraine," my father said on the phone, probably still having not recovered from his shell shock, "if you don't wanna fight."

For some, this war helped them find meaning. For others, it has been disturbingly disorienting. Yet others have hardly noticed any change. I wonder how these Bukovinian lads, back then, were making sense of what was happening to them, how they explained this war to themselves when receiving a summons and when deployed to their positions, when they were being shelled, and when they were delivered to the hospital. Did they think of their wives, European values, the molding of the nation, personal freedom, or the three hundred years of Russian colonialism? I wonder, but I cannot know. I do hope, though, that they are still alive.

6

Know Thine Enemy

MARTA HAIDUCHOK

More than two years into the war, the Ukrainian socials are overflowing with emotional phrases threatening the enemy, such as "Rusni pyzda," ("Fuck all Russians") and, "A good Russian is a dead Russian," as well as desperate statements suggesting that even our children will have to continue killing Russians. Against a backdrop of Russian missile terror, social media users ponder whether "seven-year-old Marina Smirnova from Moscow is personally guilty of the war?" and almost univocally answer yes, while Telegram channels celebrate each new deadly strike in Belgorod. Everyone with a Russian passport is found guilty, regardless of their stance. For a part of Ukrainian society, the duality of belligerents transcends the realm of the war effort and becomes a matter of personal strife. This affect became a media cliché, and then a political statement, which later turned into a particular type of war effort carried out intimately. The dissemination of hatred over the last two years is explicable. However, what still requires examination is the changing character of wartime political action focusing on the image of the enemy.

The fear of Russian influence existed in Ukraine before the full-scale invasion, and yet the strategy of overcoming this fright with conscious aversion emerged recently. In 2021, Ukrainian right-wing activist Serhii Sternenko proclaimed, "Our Russophobia is not enough." On February 24, 2022, he added: "It must become Russohatred. The occupants must die." The latter expression, which was too long to remain a slogan, was shortened to its original form and gained popularity only after the actual object of the statement entirely disappeared. "Russophobia," which initially was supposed to back the struggle against the occupiers, became an aversion to everything Russian. What follows from this sentiment is neither militant resistance nor fearless confrontation. It focuses more on the eviction of "Russian traces."

Many young Ukrainian civilians have never met Russians. They probably never experienced personally brutal Russification, unlike their parents or grandparents, or else they live too far away to experience the territorial proximity. The context of less Russified Western Ukraine thus confronts the central and eastern regions for their cultural and oftentimes linguistic assimilation to the Russian world. Unable to exercise their hate in direct interaction, they turned to what was close, and those Ukrainians who were not performatively displaying their hatred toward Russians become equated with the enemy. Differentiation from all things Russian in newsfeeds and social milieus frequently verges on digital violence, stalking, and threats, transforming into a hunt for "bad Ukrainians"—those who most resemble the enemy.

The hunt for "bad Ukrainians" is a practical differentiation mechanism to detect the internal enemy. On the battlefield, unlike in civil life, the enemy is supposed to be easily identified and marked with a flag or uniform. The symbols that create a nation, such as language, tradition, history, and sometimes even appearance, are insufficient when the enemy might behave just like you. What happens if someone were to be misidentified as the enemy? What if the enemy and a friend behave and look alike? In the pre-2014 world, Russian and Ukrainian spaces were more intertwined, and those questions did not often emerge. Ukrainians fear resembling the enemy because the similarity appears once the distinct differences, such as language, are eliminated. In the words of René Girard, the antagonists become doubles. For a part of Ukrainian society, this is equal to the victory of Putinism; the specter of "fraternal nations," where there is no Ukraine specifically autonomous from an elder-brother Russia, might become too real, rendering "Ukrainianness" extinct. This phobia is based on the fear of losing the characteristics of oneself, being unable to distinguish the enemy from the friend, "them" from "us."

A recognizable enemy whose affiliation with the other side is clear does not evoke the same fear as an inconspicuous one. Performative Russophobia, in that sense, limits exposure to everything Russian and turns fear into hatred, isolation into rejection. The physical similarities between Ukrainians and Russians, as well as the similarities in what media they consume and even the dialects they speak (such as between the residents of the Kharkiv and Belgorod regions), expose the nature of this hatred. It is not toward something one cannot understand, but the opposite—a very strong disguise, because one can understand a little too much. In Sternenko's statement, Russophobia is inherently "ours" and limited only to Ukrainians. It defines "us" through the shared feeling of hatred and the society it creates. Virtue signaling produces a hermetic circle, a response to immense fear, adopted as a weapon of creating distinction where there was none. Insularity never enables knowledge.

But why would one decide to avoid the enemy instead of learning who the enemy is? What happened to knowing your enemy?

Russophobia prompts a new expression of political action focused on disengagement with the omnipresent Russian context. Faced with an unprecedented and unfathomable level of military aggression, ever more Ukrainians are adopting the deterministic and essentialist perception of the Russian population. The enemy is static and rigid—and all

Russians appear incapable of change, critical thought, and resistance. The narratives supporting these statements are popular and explicitly degrading: authoritarianism and the lack of opposition are in "their" nature; therefore, why would one try thinking and working toward a Russian democratic future? The response of the Ukrainian side is thus to prolong the isolation. Russophobia, as expressed in Sternenko's slogans, disregards the reasons or causes of war because knowing them would require closing the distance and facing the enemy. It does not concern the postwar future but continues the seclusion. Hatred encourages inaction.

Slogans that urge Ukrainians to radicalize in their hate and multiply their efforts in rejecting things Russian deny the very possibility of changing whatever is Russian, as well as what is ultimately Ukrainian. They create an artificial distinction that does not require any intervention, and thus, the activism of hate limits itself to tickling the emotions and never proceeds to gaining knowledge. What served as a functional mechanism aimed at protecting politics from antagonistic Russian influence now ends up protecting citizens from politics by justifying their inability to bring any change. Our Russophobia, indeed, is not enough—this strong feeling of disgust should be transformed into pursuit of deep knowledge of the enemy.

Part II

Solidarity

7

We Are the Embassy

YEVHEN YASHCHUK

Suppose one finds abandoned boxes stuffed with first-aid kits and power banks in a university's basement in late 2023 with the label "Oxford University Ukrainian Society" (OUUS) on them. Those supplies are ready for delivery to the war zone 1,500 miles away. The Russo–Ukrainian war has left its marks not only on the usage of university rooms but on the character of the society that uses the space. One may wonder, "What does the university have to do with a distant conflict it is not experiencing directly?" Well, the war has been on the campus from the very beginning, with the boxes being just one of those signs. Yet to make sense of the war at the university, one must first be willing to recognize its obnoxious presence.

The international university permits the activities of national student societies that offer a variety of cultural and entertainment events, and the university consistently stresses their status as student based. Immediately after the invasion, otherwise lethargic Ukrainian students turned to OUUS as a means to manifest their Ukrainian identity, and its role as a traditional students' society waned. Non-Ukrainian members of the university community and non-university people in the city referred to OUUS as a representative body that could navigate their response to war, be it a fundraiser for ambulances or organizing a city rally. Upon their arrival on campus, new Ukrainian students had to face those shifted affiliations while tacitly redefining the university's role in wartime.

The unwritten principles and written rules of international universities were designated for the peacetime campus. Unsurprisingly, universities' responses to the war are inadequate in at least two respects: first, in their treatment of students, and second, in their political engagements. While Ukrainian students instantly recognized their representative capacity and sought to act, the Oxford administration approached them individually through the customary well-being and excellence policies. Following the idea of "positive education" with its practice of care on a case-by-case basis, Oxford remained committed "to the mental health and well-being of all students." In this regard, the students' Ukrainian background mattered only insofar as there was a perceived risk to the individual's mental health. However, sticking to its peacetime guidelines, the university chose to treat these risks as temporary, as irritants that might be removed by the means of the system or at least dulled for the time one is a student. But at the end of the day, the war continues.

The Russo–Ukrainian War will surely not destroy the campus buildings in Oxford, so the administration might ignore the war out of best intentions. Nonetheless, the war affects part of the student community, and to those students, the university's political character is revealed. First and foremost, Oxford obliges itself to "foster freedom of expression within a framework of robust civility," regardless of the topic, context, and the sides involved.[9] If one voices an opinion, the university defines counter-opinion as the only legitimate reaction. Thus, the university policies provide a robust discursive framework to salvage discussion and understanding at all costs. The intellectual space for voicing contradictory opinions, however, does not completely fit the situations marked by unilateral agendas that justify the crime of war. The university that positions itself as politically global would have the capacity to bring together different but academically and morally legitimate positions for debate. That, however, would require more investment than cultivating splendid isolation. Without this institutional engagement, the students, who know too well what an existential threat is, might find it hard to come to terms with the deliberative framework that relegates many normative concerns to the background with reference to freedom of expression.

The university's exclusive focus on freedom of speech does not leave much space for maneuvering in the dialogical environments it enables. A case in point is the invitation by the prestigious Oxford Majlis debate society to Andrei Kelin, Russian ambassador to the United Kingdom, in November 2023. The Ukrainian students resisted this initiative, seeing the ambassador's presence as legitimizing the war in the "positive university." They aimed to contest the imagined balance of opinions ubiquitously supported by the institution, a balance that proved to be dysfunctional in this case. Some participants almost instantly replied, "You should have come and challenged the ambassador." The organizers appealed to the freedom of speech praised by their university to promote their event and did not consider other normative concerns, such as understanding or solidarity; unaffected university members can easily ignore the war if it does not invade the campus, and thus apply the imagined peacetime rules to their initiatives.

The Ukrainian students were left to protest Kelin's presence on their own. Their attempts to involve the Embassy of Ukraine in seeking institutional support failed because the embassy's work was almost paralyzed by the absence of an ambassador. Standing against the Russian ambassador, however, implied the responsibility to follow the procedures defined by the university, the city, and the country of their temporary residence. Members of the Ukrainian student society had to express their stance against the Russian state while preventing the amplification of the event by their action. In this situation of mixed pressures, the OUUS's members had to define their strategy, which combined both collective and individual involvement. After protesting the ambassador, the OUUS organized dozens of cultural, social, and debate-like events. Each of them was an individual student initiative that appealed to the university community and beyond, aiming to form bridges of solidarity and to engage those members of this international university who did not feel that the full-scale Russian invasion of Ukraine was "their war."

Students from Ukraine seeking relief in the international universities these days will face the war-forged core of their respective national student societies. Those are likely to be self-proclaimed representative bodies recognized by outsiders, bodies whose engagement led to the appearance of wartime supplies in student's dorms. "We are like the embassy," one of the OUUS's members cheered during a pub night. On a different pub occasion, a former member of the Embassy of Ukraine finished his speech, "You are the embassy in your university." Well, this embassy depends entirely on the students' capacity to maintain its functions. Some of those who initiated its transformations more than two years ago are still present on campus, passing along memories of what already seems to be a distant past through the rapidly changing cycle of academic years. They are also the ones who experienced altruistic solidarity from the university and city community at the beginning of Russia's full-scale invasion. However, expecting solidarity at the present moment of the war, Ukrainian students face the necessity of acknowledging and reacting to other wars, those that were there but which students ignored before February 2022 and those that started in between. It is time to understand and make new choices.

The war changed the roles, affiliations, and representation structures instituted for the international university in peacetime. For diaspora students, their brief time on campus is defined by involvement in wartime activism oriented toward their homeland. At the same time, the administration hides behind the excuse of preserving freedoms that allegedly prevent it from responding to the injustices of war. With that, the university community chooses sides either by its decisions to get engaged with one conflict and not with the other, or by its choice to abstain altogether.

War-affected students on international campuses must clarify their actions and their belonging first with themselves, then with the university organizations they are a part of, and then with the people who recognize them as connected to their country of origin. It is a marathon with a constant search for a war–life balance while probing the university's political boundaries. The institution treats students as wards, expecting them to achieve excellence in their studies abstracted from any external challenges and overwhelming extracurricular activities. One may wonder, "What is the university's social and political role during the war?" Nevertheless, some students interrupt writing their essays and return to the familiar basement. They pick up the boxes with medical supplies and dispatch them to Ukraine from a non-war-affected "positive university" in the third year of the full-scale war.

8

In Warsaw by the Sky-Carousel

ELA KWIECIŃSKA

Psychologists claim that rituals help maintain mental health. Some start their day with yoga, but I usually check the statistics of destroyed Russian tanks that the Ukrainian Army issues every morning. Well, judging by Telegram, Ukraine still stands and keeps fighting. Now I can have my morning cup of coffee. I am unsure whether I help anyone in Ukraine while checking war updates from my Warsaw apartment or when I teach Ukrainian history at a Polish university. When I asked my students why they decided to attend my seminar on nineteenth-century Ukrainian history, some mentioned that their grandparents were born in Lviv or other places under Polish rule before World War II. However, most admitted they wanted to understand their Ukrainian friends better.

Ukrainian volunteers who stayed at my place during the first weeks of the Russian invasion named our chat after the slogan of the 1944 Warsaw Uprising: "Warszawa wal-czy!" ("Warsaw fights!"). They were all young historians. Oleksii Rudenko, a PhD student at Central European University, was the one who contacted me. I first met Oleksii, his girlfriend, and their friend when I was bringing additional bedclothes from the family house to my flat, and so they stayed. Oleksii put his Euromaidan flag on one of the walls. We did not converse much but exchanged technical information about humanitarian aid and its transportation to Ukraine. During one of these talks, Oleksii asked me whether I wanted to join the Invisible University for Ukraine, and I immediately agreed. Joining IUFU seemed to be a mere prolongation of searching for helmets during our small-scale 2022 Warsaw Uprising on our common *dilo* (matter). Soon, my two-bedroom apartment became a hostel and humanitarian aid hub. It was my responsibility as a human to address the catastrophe when states or international organizations lagged—we all thought that if we did not care about the war, no one would.

Soon, my solidarity with Ukrainians seemed limited by the dimensions of my *pidloha* (floor). At one point, there was no place to put more mattresses to host more people or store more humanitarian aid packages. In spring 2022, while walking down Warsaw's streets, I looked at the buildings and thought how much empty, unused space was inside them and how many other refugees they could host—while I could not. I was angry with calm Polish people.

The most important limits are those of your loved ones. If you refuse to be a bystander, you must constantly decide who has more right to your time and space. In February 2022, I asked my little sister to leave my flat (thank you, Ania!) so that I could provide more space for Ukrainian volunteers whom I had never met before. Later, when refugees filled my place to capacity, I started asking for help from my family, friends, friends of my friends, or even strangers on Facebook groups—everyone who had spare mattresses. I hosted a Ukrainian refugee with children who turned out to be unvaccinated at my family house, risking the health of my ninety-year-old grandma. Other refugees who had been through the concentration camp in Mariupol brought bed bugs to my flat. While it was being disinfected, I moved for two months to our family house, and thankfully, my profoundly religious and conservative grandma tolerated me staying with my partner in our bed before marriage. Then, I turned my mother's basement into a warehouse so that I could store even more humanitarian aid.

I could not disappoint people who called me around the clock desperately asking for help. The fact that I am one of the few Poles who speak Ukrainian and Russian, and who also understands Ukrainian *surzhyk* (a Ukrainian-Russian dialect), is an ironic consequence of the 1990s abolition of Russian classes in Polish schools—what had been a Polish anticolonial reaction back then now hindered the ongoing Ukrainian anticolonial resistance. Hence, when the administration of the Faculty of History at the University of Warsaw would call me, saying, "Ktoś do Ciebie" ("There's someone to visit you"), I knew there was a refugee who spoke only Ukrainian or Russian. One was an elderly history professor from Eastern Ukraine who had spent several nights at the railway station. Someone explained to him where the Faculty of History was, and since he did not speak a word in any foreign language, he became "my visitor."

The boss was upset with me. I should not have left my desk to meet "visitors" and was only permitted to think about the war after five p.m.—a good citizen comes to the workplace punctually and lets the state solve humanitarian catastrophes. Later, I left the research project I was working on and started lecturing on Polish and Ukrainian modern history at the same faculty. The university launched a solidarity program for Ukrainian students but did not provide additional infrastructure or translators, so I agreed to receive even more "visitors." Care, support, and administrative work are still often delegated to the female sphere, which no one outside of it respects, either on campus or off.

My *pidloha* started to break down when I lost my non-tenured university position. I started working as an oral history researcher and recorded testimonies of Ukrainian war victims. Given my understanding of most dialects spoken in Ukraine, I felt a moral responsibility as a witness. So, to whom should I dedicate my time? Refugees telling of the hell of the war or loved ones telling of a hell in their own lives? Eventually, I ended up being alone and jobless. I'm not an indifferent bystander, and I'm not a victim—I am a helper-freak.

The loneliness and exhaustion of helpers bring back memories of World War II. The poem by Czesław Miłosz, "Campo dei Fiori," describes the sky-carousel next to the ghetto wall and Polish people enjoying themselves when Jews started the Warsaw Uprising in 1943. Miłosz looked up to the cloudless Warsaw sky, listening to the carnival tune, and compared it with the hot wind and salvos coming from the burning ghetto.[10] If the Borgesian magical mirrors of God are watching us and showing us our vain reflection, I can look straight into my mirror with no fear.[11] Yet, when I look at my Ukrainian friends and students from IUFU, their heroic resilience keeps me humbled.

9

Synchronized with the Future

BALÁZS TRENCSÉNYI

We should not overestimate ourselves.
—Lesia Ukrainka, *Cassandra*

Whether from within or without, it is impossible to experience the totality of a war. Every point of observation—be it spatial or temporal—one might assume is necessarily relational, and the only totality one might experience in this context—but can hardly transmit to others—is that of one's own death. Thus, even total war is necessarily partial, implying different experiences for different participants. This does not mean, however, that sharing these partial, situated experiences is impossible. Some might be shared right away, while others by default divide or even fragment the respective community.

The current Ukrainian war experience comes with many synchronous and asynchronous layers. Neither your mother tongue, your passport, nor where you are from and where you are now implies automatic involvement or noninvolvement in the war. A "nation at war" is always figurative—it refers to an imagined community that is reconstituted every moment from many perspectives, a matrix of partly divergent, partly converging elective affinities. Even if you are not personally threatened by missiles in this very moment, even if you are not even in Ukraine, you are "in-war" because you feel and act in a way that posits you as part of a we-in-war. This, by necessity, also blurs to a certain extent the position of the so-called outsider: even if I am not personally threatened by missiles, if I have not crossed the border of Ukraine since 2019, even if I did not "enter" the war, the war entered me. I am in-war because you are in-war.

Still, these two modalities are not identical. Irrespective of outsiders' cultural competence, their engagement with the national community remains at the level of participant observation, which exposes the need to be tactful and humble. That is, as an outsider, I cannot tell you whom to hate or whom not to hate, whether to leave or to remain, to fight or hide, to speak out or fall silent. At the same time, my commitment and the experience of synchronizing entails also investing one's full personality. I cannot be partially in-war, with half of my mind for myself only. I cannot avoid thinking about, reading about, talking about, and even eventually judging hatred, diaspora, mobilization, or public debates in

Ukraine. But I also carry my own battles and defeats, some of them reaching back before you were born.

For some time, I thought that this was Europe against the ghost of totalitarianism, following the reverberating slogan that Ukraine is fighting for Europe ("For our liberty and for yours," as the Polish Romantic insurgents would have it), paradoxically saving it to be able to be part of it—with all the civilizational and material benefits attributed to such an exclusive membership. But I saw enough of the crisis of liberal democratic politics in my native Hungary after it entered the European Union to have second thoughts about this secular eschatology of liberal democratic convergence. As we talked more, I came to accept that rather than these lofty moral and geopolitical considerations, the finality of the war is mere survival, both individual and collective ("national"—with all the caveats linked to using this abstraction). Even if there is tension or sometimes even a tragically irresolvable contradiction between these two normativities, survival means an open future.

An open future is a rare commodity in our world, as we are experiencing an atemporalization—losing touch with the sequence of past–present–future and gradually sinking into an eternal present. Our politicians promise to defend us from deterioration, collapse, and the decomposition of our social, economic, ecological, and cultural habitat, but rarely if at all formulate any vision of the future in terms of collective agency. We are lucky if they do not themselves generate the crisis from which they promise to defend us. At the same time, the political ideologies sustaining liberal democracy after WWII (at least in Western Europe) were linked to a vision of an open future both in their socialist, liberal, and Christian Democratic iterations. My war is thus also about recovering the futural modalities of politics, of going beyond the restorative position that seeks merely to preserve or reconstruct what is being lost.

I do not know what Ukraine will or should look like after the war, but listening to you, I am convinced that it cannot and will not be merely the replica of what it was before February 24, 2022. My war, which is your war and not your war at the same time, is not about recovering what was lost, no matter how horrible these losses are, but about recovering the indeterminacy of the future. Indeterminacy is not equal to contingency. The experience of the Invisible University (a daily plebiscite where students vote by investing their intellectual and emotional energy) is precisely about this: talking and mostly listening, becoming conscious of the responsibility we all share for the future.

That said, in a modern war, our individual actions and projections can hardly change the general course of history, and even the 900 students we had the pleasure to work with represent an infinitesimal fraction of the Ukrainian society in war. Rather than changing the big picture, my war is about creating spaces of dialogue: sharing moments of despair, the pleasure of thinking together, witnessing, and contributing to the birth of new ideas. It is thus both direct and indirect, thinking through and experiencing through. Perhaps a bit also of acting through. It is about our future. But I should never forget that the indeterminacy of war has a dark side, one we cannot overcome with any collective futural projection, inherent to the fragility and finality of individual human existence: when saying goodbye after the first summer school in July 2022, it struck me that perhaps it would be the last time we met.

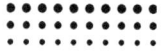

10

war meets war

KATIA LYSENKO

the war that is happening has happened in ukraine twice. once in 2014, and in 2022, it happened for the second time. one war happened twice.

"during the training at the polygon we're constantly getting blown up on the training mines. the instructor says the problem is we walk too much like civilians" (day 17).[12] when war happens the human gait changes, a different grip on the ground. the ground is lost under one's feet. if one continues walking upright—the gravitational center shifts and the head becomes the fulcrum. yet if not, some humans still do not fall down and do not fly away. something is holding them onto nothing, and the grip is tight. this is the war gait—humans' walking on nothing and holding to it tightly.

war happened for the first time for everyone already. it happened as a fact, as an actualized possibility of war. the actualized possibility of war is the ongoing war. we are all at war. yet the war that is happening does not lead to the war that is fought. the latter war is not derived from the former one. people are murdered in ukraine every day, and new heroes enter eternity, not closing doors after themselves.

—wait, all these wars look familiar.

—no. every war is new, and new people do what has been done many times before.

—there is no war other than the first and the last.

something is happening, but it is not an experience yet. the second happening of war is war experience, which happens through the person. time is required for these two instances of war happening to meet—more than seven days if a person is not a god. a person needs some "after," which does not imply "after happening" or "after war," and is bound to "after in-happening." in this "after" we experience what we experience, according to all possible physical and psychic constellations. time with "after" meets war—time with "no after."

death is always the first and the last, and it's never delayed. every murder in war is the advent of war, and those who are alive have their "after" for the second happening to experience the death of others. and people are murdered in war; that is what i know about it. people are responsible for war in its first happening, and people are responsible for their experience in its second happening. i do not know what happened with many people who died or were murdered in the last decade. i know, for sure, that my aunt vita is sitting on the cloud with her cigarette that she lights from the sun, but i do not know about others. i know that human death is irreversible. "some advice: don't be a hero, for fuck's sake" (day 18).

—you can't bring anything back, there's no one able to help it.

—yes, granny. dead people are dead people.

some people who are not dead have their time with "after" to learn the commerce of experience. they equalize experiences and believe they can be stored as a possession. they also believe that their possession has a particular function: for every X who experiences Y, the Y is capitalized into Z according to the current experience exchange rate. thus, Y is experienced not in the first and the last time. one can store more Z than the other. a person becomes a sum and is judged as a sum: the more, the better. other people who have their time with "after" acquire experience without storing it because it is a qualitative change for them. the "latter" experience of war does not determine the "former" one that happened a decade ago and vice versa—there is no hierarchy. their qualitative experience is concrete and total, as the happening is always concrete and total. the accumulation of experience obliges us to nothing—for better or worse.

—katia, i just thought that my grandchildren might be speaking german…

—mama, they might not exist at all.

time with "after" is present for those people who store the quantified experience and acquire the qualitative experience only if they are either safe and/or have weapons to fight.

"you just need to learn to kill from a safe place. and write your will. it's not a joke at all" (day 18). because a human can be murdered and cannot be resurrected. "today we got our weapons. the automatic rifle and pistol were in storage for many decades. did the dude who covered my pistol in oil in 1950 think who would be rubbing it off and in what circumstances?" (day 8).

the war gait manifests the tension of the first and the last happenings. if we stay in the first happening, the actualized possibility of war, there is no tension but a clutch. when we stay in the second happening, which is experience, there is not enough traction. maybe a human is merely the one who holds onto nothing and tightly. "i'm flipping through the social networks, but i don't react. this is it—the limit. i had enough for seven months. it's not a bad reserve of strength, isn't it."[13] any step—any ethical choice—is a total choice, a choice not between more or less, but a choice of another. it is not about something being a much better or less-worse one. "we're getting dressed in the green protective 'elephant' suits. you can feel the sweat of the previous cadets on your fingers, the thick black rubber is warm and damp" (day 11). it soaks a lot, but how much, how much more? everything that is the first and the last is concrete and total.

—what is it, and how is it?

—i am a bit dead.

—maybe a bit more?

helping another person does not imply understanding them. there is no necessity in understanding. just people. here faces go to hell, and everyone is so busy saving them. we do not need the same motivation to fight. "then the instructor unties it, says: 'good job, you endured!' what did i endure? i knew it was fake" (day 22). we should put all our efforts into not the second happening but the first—understanding what is happening regardless of how it is experienced. everything can be lost in a day. the face is just a derivative of all possible circumstances—deeds, thoughts, and valid documents. some are more appealing to one, some less, but human is not a sum. "training didn't accomplish anything. i'm already big enough to understand that motivation is a personal matter" (day 3).

—would you be so kind as to stop understanding me?

reality is not something we enter, it is what we do. it does not belong to one human and is not made by one person. war is happening, and we all are captured in war. some adjust to war and experience it through explanations. they make up not the first and not the last war but their war experience. "and so the cities grow more and more empty. this is how 'your own truth' defines the shared absurdity for all of us."[14]

we know that nothing ever repeats and everything happens anew, so to say, "everything is new" is to say, "everything is as always." a mortal human meets another mortal human, hi there. one particular human meets another particular human. war is not necessary for this meeting—it is not necessary for anything. but when the war is already happening, they have to meet twice. the first time their meeting is a fact, and the second time it is a step. "fresh scars carved up his face, his gaze absent. he's learning to walk all over again, and he has one goal: to get from point A to point B" (day 15). again, and for the first time, a particular human learns to walk upright, holding onto nothing. the first and the last human.

11

Stronger Together

MAKSYM SNIHYR

In 2024, during his traditional New Year's address, President Volodymyr Zelenskyi pointed out the choice that a Ukrainian citizen, whether male or female, must make. Putting himself in the place of a fellow Ukrainian, Zelenskyi concluded: "I know that one day I will have to ask myself, 'Who am I?' To make a choice about who I want to be. A victim or a winner? A refugee or a citizen? And everyone knows the answer. And the answer is Ukraine. Because Ukrainians are stronger together. So it's time to be together!"

Back in 2019, President Zelenskyi expressed his wish to attract people of Ukrainian origin living abroad back to the country and promised them citizenship. Five years later, as his New Year's speech testifies, he returned to the idea of gathering Ukrainian people on the territory of Ukraine—this time in completely different circumstances. Against the backdrop of Russia's full-scale aggression, Zelenskyi called on Ukrainians to be stronger than their fear and stronger than their doubts and return to their native land. Considered this way, "Ukrainians" are not merely people of Ukrainian origin. Neither are they only those who hold a Ukrainian passport, wherever war might find them. Rather, they are Ukrainian citizens guided by the call to return. In an era when information moves easily and quickly across borders, Ukrainian citizenship becomes territorial. One is not born but becomes "Ukraine" only with a passport in hand and feet on the ground.

The new mobilization law, "On Amendments to Certain Legislative Acts of Ukraine on Certain Issues of Military Service, Mobilization and Military Registration," was adopted in the spring of 2024. It sets specific conditions for issuing passports and providing consular services to any male, able-bodied Ukrainian citizen aged 18–60 and residing outside the country. The Ukrainian Ministry of Foreign Affairs released a ministerial letter implementing this limitation a month before the law came into force. Defending this decision, Minister Dmytro Kuleba stated, "What it looks like now: a man of conscription age went abroad, showed his state that he does not care about its survival, and then comes and wants to receive services from this state. It does not work this way. Our country is at war." The minister decided to "restore fair attitudes toward men of conscription age in Ukraine and abroad," reminding citizens of their duties. This decision received warm praise among those who demanded equal redistribution of the war burden. One of the Ukrainian bloggers known for his active participation in the war effort wrote that the minister did a great job.

The strategy of the Ukrainian government is to get able-bodied men back into the country under the pretext of obtaining a military identification (ID). This ID is now issued only in Ukraine, and without it, one cannot receive any consular services. More important, one cannot apply for a passport renewal abroad. And even though, after May 18, the Ukrainian state established an electronic military ID called Reserv+, the fluctuating policy on military registration does not totally relieve those living abroad from having to choose between being a citizen or a refugee. The new mobilization law makes male citizens' return to their homeland almost unavoidable and their departure from the country rather difficult. This is how the law activates duty as a subject of international politics.

The State Security Service of Ukraine (SSU) asserts that Russian intelligence services have spent approximately $1.5 billion on psychological warfare that aims to undermine our nation's morale. The antidote SSU recommends against the psychological poison of the enemy is always undeniably strong—"Our society needs unity." Our diplomats are thus advised to do their best to help people "get together" by bringing our Ukrainian citizens back home. Meanwhile, everyday Ukrainians and the state apparatus perceive each other with mutual skepticism. On the one hand, people wonder why

Ukrainians abroad who help sustain the war effort with fund-raising, remittance, and donations are rejected by the state apparatus. On the other hand, the state tends to approach these citizens abroad with suspicion, as if all of them prefer to remain comfortable and safely away from the war. Moreover, embassy workers treat these citizens' routine issues as distractions from the more important work of representing Ukraine abroad and from the declared priority of protecting their homeland. The law addresses some of these frictions, and while applauded by some, it is unpopular among others.

Ukrainian journalist Danylo Mokryk was among those who felt compelled to share his opinion on the Ministry of Foreign Affairs decision. Mokryk urged his YouTube audience to think about the definition of "ours" (*свої*). Invoking Benedict Anderson and his idea of imagined communities, Mokryk discussed the feeling of belonging. He said that a Ukrainian passport alone does not make people "ours." And if those abroad renounce this passport in response to the new limitations, it would not be much of a loss for the nation. Seeing the absurdity of these claims, he immediately back-tracked this position, highlighting that "obviously, not all Ukrainian citizens abroad are like that." Mokryk's original statement runs counter to the position of the Ukrainian government, which increasingly aims to constrain Ukrainians to the country's territory. At the same time, the government moved toward Mokryk's position by "restoring" fair attitudes toward men of conscription age.

Staying abroad definitely does not relieve us of our duties to the homeland. And fulfilling these duties requires strength. A Ukrainian passport alone, however, does not help you overcome fears and doubts, and, as the president put it in his speech, it does not turn you into the kind of Ukrainian whom "the enemies truly fear a lot." Whether you are inside or outside Ukraine, a passport does not turn you into a victim or a winner. Yet it is the lack of it that may turn a Ukrainian from citizen to refugee, cutting the very last tie to the homeland during a time when, as President Zelenskyi reminded us, Ukrainians are stronger together. Therefore, it is time to honor the complexity of what unity might mean. Stripping any fellow citizen's consular services and refusing to renew able-bodied Ukrainian men's passports is wrong, for it will only widen divisions.

12

Neither Exiles, Nor Émigrés

OSTAP SEREDA

One of the expected consequences of war is the exile of intellectuals and the emergence of a new generation of émigrés. With the arrival of the Digital Age, the communicative space became less defined by international borders, yet the recent wars of the twenty-first century again resulted in the appearance of new communities of intellectual exiles harbored at major Western academic centers. Many Ukrainian scholars and students, both those who were outside Ukraine on February 24, 2022, and those who crossed the Ukrainian border and joined them later, can also be seen as a new community of the "war exiles," separate from the friends and colleagues who are staying in Ukraine. However, the experience of the Invisible University for Ukraine suggests the opposite.

The alarming nighttime news of the full-scale Russian military invasion reached me and my family in the university town of Jena in Germany, where we were staying at Imre Kertész Kolleg. Although the contrast between peaceful life in European towns and the images of destroyed Eastern Ukrainian cities became unbearably surreal, online spaces and social media helped us maintain immediate contact with friends, relatives, and colleagues. My home university, the Ukrainian Catholic University (UCU) in Lviv, invited me to join the internet-based sessions and prayers that sustained the illusion of extraterritoriality, although nobody could ignore striking differences conditioned by location. In Lviv, the UCU campus became a hub for volunteer activities, helping refugees from Eastern Ukrainian cities and the Ukrainian Army. Almost every day, my colleagues and students had to shelter themselves from the threat of missile attacks. Those who were outside of the country, in places where life seemingly continued as usual, were expected to undertake the role of intellectual ambassadors of Ukraine and to mobilize international support.

War enforces uniformity also in the intellectual sphere, and the idea of speaking in one voice as the most effective way of influencing international audiences began to prevail. Previously, we tried to avoid speaking in an academic context about "us" as a national community. Now, from the first days of the war, I was often expected to speak to various audiences on behalf of all Ukrainians, and it seemed more challenging than to speak from an academic distance. I had to learn how to combine the empathetic view of an insider and the critical approach of a reflective analyst under new wartime conditions. The IUFU classes that started in April helped me regain balance. Although the students shared an intense sense of societal solidarity and responsibility, they preserved intellectual autonomy and an interest in open discussions. Speaking in one voice, however righteous, would block the urgent search for answers demanded by the war. In addition to Ukrainian colleagues, IUFU online classes were taught by dozens of international instructors who demonstrated that the Ukrainian case is important for rethinking the established conceptual schemes worldwide. Many Ukrainian scholars and students were willing to blame Western academia for ignoring the danger of Russian imperialism, reducing the East European borderlands to insignificant peripheral zones of imperial centers, and depriving them of agency and voice. However, international colleagues who expressed solidarity with us by joining our classes also shared some of these concerns with the Russocentric bias of Western academia, thus, the dividing line between Ukrainian and non-Ukrainian intellectuals became unimportant. However, the invisible hierarchy of Western-centered academy did not disappear automatically; sometimes, we still hope that our Western colleagues will have ready answers for us.

The search by Ukrainian intellectuals for both recognition and intellectual inspiration from the West did not begin in 2022, but the promotion of Ukrainian studies abroad became one of the priorities of Ukrainian society and government only recently. This shift to the humanities and social sciences resembled previous moments in Ukrainian modern history when academia seemed to play the role of the leading national institution. Parallels with the Cold War period appeared obvious, yet the differences were tremendous. After World War II, hundreds of Ukrainian scholars and students found themselves on the Western side of the Iron Curtain and undertook the mission of a diasporic community—to preserve and represent cultural heritage and national scholarship and to expose Soviet crimes abroad. Any ties with the Soviet-controlled homeland were severed, and visits behind the curtain were rare. The most dynamic and open-minded of Ukrainian scholars-in-exile aspired to earn a recognizable place in mainstream Western academia, but they often found themselves marginalized in the traditionalist "ethnic" part of the academic spectrum.

The collapse of the Soviet Union in 1991 seemed a moment of triumph for Ukrainian studies in the West, but a handful of scholars was not enough to retain global intellectual attention. The focus of international academia quickly shifted from the post-Soviet space to other regions, leaving the Ukrainian complex of invisibility unchallenged. However, numerous networks and research centers facilitated the engagement of Ukrainian scholarship with global academia, helping the postindependence intellectual discussions become diverse, dynamic, and to involve a broader segment of society. The growing role in Ukrainian studies of those scholars who did not share a Ukrainian background crucially reduced intellectual isolation. Several heated exchanges among historians challenged the radical nationalist narratives of heroic memory or national victimhood. Today, the extent to which this promising atmosphere can be preserved and sustained during the war and afterward, when intellectuals in Ukraine are overwhelmed by a sense of duty to sustain civil unity and resilience, is an open question.

Many new academic programs that were initiated after February 2022 out of a sense of political solidarity with Ukraine, including the Invisible University for Ukraine, created new conditions for the internationalization of Ukrainian humanities and social sciences. A "Western" affiliation became a standard part of many Ukrainian academic CVs, although martial law significantly limited the mobility of male Ukrainian scholars across the border. Nevertheless, academic circulation never stopped, and thousands of Ukrainian colleagues and students combine international scholarly involvement while preserving their presence in their home institutions.

In this situation, online programs such as IUFU allow scholars outside the country to stay integrated in Ukrainian academia and students studying abroad to engage with their peers. They facilitate the immediate presence of those abroad in discussions and projects at home (and vice versa). This arrangement helps prevent a separate émigré academic sphere from forming, thus limiting brain drain. It also overcomes the traditional institutional inertia of academic life in Ukraine and creates more space for individual initiatives and agency. On the other hand, the close connection to Western academia helps students learn about its current dynamics, conflicts, and crises from within.

The new generation of Ukrainian intellectuals should be shaped not only by their resilience to war challenges but also by their ability to produce change. The first fruits of the expected conceptual shifts can be observed already. In the aftermath of World War II, Ukrainian refugees usually shared social space with their Eastern European counterparts and tended to think within that box, arguing that their national expertise provided the key to understanding the whole of Eastern Europe. Today the global dimension is dominating, and our students endeavor to move beyond the conceptual limits of regionally defined area studies.

Thus, contrary to the divisive impact of wartime conditions, the community evolving out of our IUFU classes cannot be divided into those inside and those outside of the country, but rather reinforces the sense of solidarity, mutual support, and intellectual openness. It is not that differences in experiences, sometimes significant, are ignored. In fact, our students are increasingly reflexive about their and others' positionality, but in a much more complex setting of identities and belonging.

I continue to teach online students of the UCU and IUFU, now from Berlin. Sometimes, I even combine these classes, as the UCU is one of the institutional partners of the IUFU and recognizes the credits that students receive from CEU. Like many of my colleagues who are now abroad, I feel from time to time that we are almost following the steps of famous Ukrainian émigré scholars from the postwar epoch, but obviously, our path is quite different. We are neither exiles nor émigrés.

Part III

Endurance

13

We Who Were Living
Are Now Dying

GUILLAUME LANCEREAU AND
TETIANA ZEMLIAKOVA

There is nothing new in war except for the humanity it surprises and the humans it forces to fight. We did not initiate this war. We did not prepare offensive plans, recruit soldiers, or conduct drills. Yet, we made this war and accepted it as ours. We engendered it—it has our faces and bodies, and then, for us, "being at war" and "living our times" became one.

#

The progress promised by the historical era seemed to be well underway when the unexpected disaster occurred, compelling the flood of modernity to disappear for the benefit of humankind. We immediately sensed the noxious effluvia of history contradicting itself. Indeed, our species had grown a specific organ responsible for the perception of time, which was inherent to historical time only, sensing and judging our times, detecting the pressure of the inevitable, decomposing things into imaginable and unimaginable, registering the flows of necessity, and tying our every glimpse of life to history. When the inconceivable war began and dared to continue against all odds, ruining our expectations of perpetual flourishing, we knew that history betrayed us. Still, there was no way to escape, no way to rectify its wrongful path or restore its broken promises.

#

For months, we gawked in amazement, feared becoming extinct, and kept reciting our rosary: this war is impossible; it is not from our political realm, and it is, therefore, the work of a madman—or worse, a pure catastrophe. The war made us wander between obsessive denial and apocalyptic fever. In the beginning, there was mechanized death marching through the fields, and we accepted it as we resigned ourselves to weather changes—we faced it with indignation and dignity. Certainly, reasons for pride and satisfaction emerged from time to time, alongside acts of solidarity: wheat-azure flags on façades, rallies in public squares, minutes of silence, poignant proclamations, as well as refined pains inflicted on those witnessing distant atrocities. None of these excitements could suspend our apraxia, no matter how we feared losing our sanity. Our impulses unfolded in brief bursts unrelated to one another—a succession of instants, deprived of overarching vision. As the war continued, our bodies slowly adapted to their poisoned environment. We learned to breathe shallowly, not to inhale dreadful odors; we learned to read the signs of time as personal sorrows and private revelations, and soon, the face of war became our only mask. We transmuted outrage into grief or austere acceptance of martyrdom and embraced the imperative of endurance, seeking the reasons for spiritual elegance in catastrophe. Meanwhile, our times demanded that we not sacrifice our humanity. Preserving this dignity—by bearing arms or cursing them—became the only mode of contact with the war we deemed agreeable. One way of exercising it was to persevere in the prewar normality in which war had seemed impossible. The war invaded more and more spheres of life, but we continued our search for places where we could pretend to live as we did before. As around the year one thousand, the sense of the imminence of the last Judgment faded: the urge to settle on earth, within the duties of the age, triumphed over contempt for the world. The war found us busy; it saw us agitated, ticking off one by one the great tasks of the day. Anchored in a gripping reality, we found normality in sustaining our biological and affective burdens.

#

Betrayed by history, we remained loyal to it, for we knew nothing of life beyond it. Modern humans are the only creatures of history. It was history that created us and soon became our environment, the only natural habitat favorable to our nutrition, betterment, and growth. For us, history is neither time past nor a horizon holding the past condensed. It is eternally present—one cannot exceed it without risking their life. We did not risk. Our present amounted to the never-ending end of history—not because time ran out or because the initial creative impulse dissipated into the dense matter that paves the universe. History could not even end, for there was no one to prophesize anything new coming after it. The new does not belong to our time and its inertia; it is untimely, irreducible to the properties of time prevalent among contemporaries who know history all too well. Our natural habitat has become uninhabitable, and we are dying with it, and this death seems so natural, just like history itself.

#

"We have carefully considered everything," said the last Voice from Above. After all, was the war anything else but the continuation of history by other means? In past deportations, partitions, and occupations, we found duties and reasons to keep fighting as we eternally had. We sought alternative salvation in scholarship and plunged into disorderly explorations of the Kyivan Rus', the religious union of 1596, and Maidan. Yet, neither body, mind, nor soul found true calm. We ended up surrounded by ghosts, products of our abstract thinking. None of these historical illuminations could disturb our agnosia: all things that war had seized and changed remained as mysterious as before.

Alarmed by the mistakes and wanderings of history on the road of progress, we wanted to know nothing of the species' own mistakes and wanderings. Rather than looking at ourselves, we held up a mirror to history for it to inspect its false tendencies, its guilty conscience toward its own leanings, its authentic character. We welcomed the war with a pyramid that resembled an enormous tower in its height and width, a new Tower of Babel composed of seven hundred thousand histories of Ukraine, eighteen million political sociologies of modern Russia, and four hundred historical anthropologies of the Eastern fringes. When we grow tired of appeasing and honoring war with history, that great incubator of dreams, we shall set fire to this dreadful mass as an expiatory sacrifice offered to truth, common sense, and true taste. Then, we will barely emerge from the most humiliating era of humanity—a humanity shrunk to the measure of its knowledge, lessened by its sole desire to know itself, reduced to looking at itself through the war in the hope of discovering something, anything about itself. Once free from our historical urges, we will no longer seek to know whether "we live in the interwar period" or in one of the first two "world wars," as we will not lie by calling the war in Ukraine the "first war on the European continent in seventy years." With new correspondences, new images, and more abundant and tragic lies, there will be no more founding events, no universal prism by which to measure the world's happening—and no more statues to topple, for ours will be taken out and put back in depending on the weather, a reverie from the day before, a bet won.

#

When it is all over, politics will become a physiognomy of the future. There will be no more war to wage, for everyone will recognize its hideous traits at the first call to arms. When another madman initiates war, no one will show up on the battlefield except to tear him into pieces. There will be no more confusion between things that affect the future, those that affect nothing, and those that are barely things. There will be only urgencies and their hierarchies. There will be no time left for day-to-day scandals, for meaningless affairs, no problem of language or positionality, no problem of art, for there will be no urge to articulate and denounce, as the art of wartime—a brave art, filled with strength, bearer of great truths, that is, great ugliness—articulated and denounced the war without thinking of warless life. There will be no problem of truth, for life always requires new lies. The war made us align true and false judgments with equal melancholy: that of the hesitant, forced into assurance; that of the ignorant, forced into expertise. Instead, we will resolve to assert everything and its opposite with equal joy, to lie better so we no longer have to pray so poorly.

#

We contemplate our prayers of yore: "War, please deign not to exist." We weigh our impotence, our libations: "State, please

106

deign to tell War not to exist." We contemplate our prayers, and we will change gods. We will change gods and disrobe believers with their unachievable empathy and their craving for transparency. Their lies cost us tears at the time when we valued all judgments only to the extent that they belonged to us and reflected our condition—our only source of faith—making the last Judgment sound like a syncopated report of personal experience. When we renounce the forces that moved us, the very idea of force, and its haruspices, there will be no entrails left from which to decipher a probable destiny, coupled with a character and inclinations. We already look at our bonds and find them hideous. We stare at our probable flight, possible death, and find ourselves unloved, unloving—for we still live among ghosts.

#

Our exodus from the perishing modernity demands other principles of vision—other hallucinations. For a long time, we had vacillated between an old man's boredom, eager to uncover familiar signs in every new thing, and our childish candor, ecstatic about each return of the same, as long as it announced itself under the trumpets of the new. But things old and things new are not meant to be stared at frivolously, for they should be devisaged.

#

Certain eras do not live up to their urgency; they come to believe that time itself accelerates. They show agitation where rest is needed and get rest where they should make haste. It is the essence of wartime to make all thinking about peace untimely. So far, all hearers of ghosts remain busy discussing how to end the war that all of them continue and which past examples of war-ending would serve as a better analogy to their scenarios. The war happened to us, and we lived through it with dignity, yet not understanding a thing—the weather was bad, the air was miasmatic, and we were cautious not to open windows for too long. Our ability to act dissolved in the reminiscences of the prewar past and anticipation of its postwar reconstruction. We believe that peace will happen to us just as the war did, and we believe that history will come to its senses, for the end cannot last forever: war, fortunately, will have been nothing more than a crisis, a disturbing disease, that lasted only as long as a quick astronomical revolution. Yet our times last until the future is invented, just as war will last until peace is conceived. War does not end, it is peace that begins—and we hope for a bang, not a whimper.

#

Today, we turn our inward eye upon ourselves; we dissect our bodies and extract their fluids. We are neither captured by war nor consumed or enslaved by it. We are ceaselessly doing this war that should never have existed and take responsibility for its ending as well. The only future peace is the one where the present war is made impossible, which is why we so desperately inspect its dark matter. We will not begin peace by mastering the morals of past apocalypses, but by leaping through the objectified knowledge and personal experience that kept us irresolute for years. We will bring face-to-face the distortions and corruptions that war imposes upon things with the transformations proper for possible peace. Timeliness is about inertia, deducibility, and direct conformity—our peace would be untimely. Just as the historical era, the war will not end by itself—it will not end until we begin the peace we cannot yet conceive. At some point in our hallucinations, we will notice the mask of war standing right where our face once was and carve it out. We see our times clearly, and we shall betray them for the future to happen.

14
Transfiguratio

OLHA STASIUK

In the beginning, there was pain.

It pierced sharply and then remained dull but ever-present. It seemed to infiltrate soil and trees, buildings and human beings, seeping into every cell of one's body, filling them like vessels, gathering in deep and hurtful pools, and stopping normal breathing and thinking. Pain transmuted us into something else. Temporarily or permanently, pain over-powered us, and we became pain.

And then, there was grief.

Actually, much more. There was strange, uncontrollable laughter, dark and intoxicating humor, and anger, which made our muscles tense and our chests ready to explode. There was sorrow, aching and never going away, and a heart-breaking sympathy followed by warm sadness of consola-tion, by the bright and empowering feeling of unity. Then, we collapsed again because of misunderstanding and mistrust that made us coarse and broken as the concrete ruins outside our windows, that pushed us into hollow tiredness, that gave us delusional and fluttery hope, and finally—despair. New experiences ground us into pieces, whether they happened to us, our close ones, or those whom we never knew: hearing the air-raid sirens, missile explosions, and cries under the rubble; seeing shot-through cars and fires at the electricity stations; reacting to harsh sounds, feeling brokenness, shallowness, fear; learning to live in immediacy with countless flags on the graves, occupation, torture, loss, death. For civilians who were deeply involved in the war, it was impossible to remain the same without the innermost transformation. Yet, we could never evaluate this change and merely grasped the symptoms, which often caught us by surprise and left us wondering who we are now. We noticed how we changed when interacting with others—hurting or healing them. Thus, our speech changed: how we spoke and what we were speaking about. In the beginning, there was pain, and because of pain, we wanted to speak.

So, have you noticed how differently you speak?

War came with its artificial, rigid, metallic language.

We learned how to refer to the weapons that killed us and protected us, how to recognize life-threatening conditions, and how to choose among life-saving medical supplies, ammunition, and equipment that we sent to our loved ones on the front line. The ground, however, was prepared. Already since 2014, we gathered the elements of this alien language: *бригада, котел, кіборги, фронт, поранений, загинув*, constituting a triggering appendix of our lives, depending on how much we were involved in the hybrid war.[15] Nonetheless, this supplementary glossary was not enough when the war invaded our lives at full scale. Our pain demanded to be shared.

I remember that during the spring of 2022, I answered every foreigner's question, "How are you?" asked in a PhD lab, by naming the types of missiles launched on Ukrainian cities and recounting every movement of the front line. Soon, I realized I lacked words and borrowed those that seemed appropriate from the black-and-white captions in books on World War I and World War II. We applied terms like "shelling" and "air raid," not knowing whether they suited the war of 2022, and later developed our vocabulary with "unmanned aerial vehicle" or "ballistics," connecting the dreadful terms with reportage pictures and memes just as children use their ABC books.

Learning how to describe the war was not enough. Pain could not sit idle; it demanded that we do something. We added vocabulary and gestures for endless funerals and learned to kneel in front of a funeral convoy or light a flare in farewell to activists killed on the front line; we accustomed ourselves to verbalizing living through trauma, providing protection, and being compassionate in times of horror. Volunteering enriched our vocabulary even more: we had to swiftly specialize in fundraising, mechanics and logistics, emergency medicine, and tactical combat casualty care, routinely deciphering hundreds of unfamiliar words wrongly spelled on dirty boxes of humanitarian aid. We decided to learn, but there was never a choice; eventually, we majored and graduated in war language. We became natural to war, and that is why we can last at least a bit longer.

Our bodies were urged to preserve themselves while enduring the unbearable, and sometimes they rebelled against words, recoiled from everyone, and we became mute with grief. Grief could come anytime, whether triggered by pictures or by faces in a crowd mistaken for the ones you would never see again. Pain demanded understanding; grief knew that it could not be understood. Eventually, we also learned how to grieve without falling apart. We developed a bizarre, new meaning of the word *okay*: it became so basic that it hurt, how basic it was. In the end, *okay* meant being alive. If you are alive, you are more okay than many others. This new meaning of *okay* gradually destroyed our loved ones and ourselves because we missed the signs of exhaustion and symptoms of unprocessed grief, despair, and even mental illness. We could save each other by noticing the changing speech—and then we could take someone's hand and say that their okay is not okay anymore—even for war.

We acquired a shell so that pain and suffering hurt us less. Then weariness took over, intensified by misunderstanding, indifference, ignorance, and callousness, which made us alienated, sometimes envious, and even bitter or cruel. We wrote vicious comments on socials and disregarded the others' pain, for it just seemed less important, as so many things did. We laughed at the outside world as only survivors can laugh in postapocalyptic nonchalance because outsiders did not sympathize enough or helped only a little. They were either spellbound by russian propaganda or busied themselves with Met Gala gowns and Eurovision glitter. In both instances, they had little relevance to our realities—they thought of themselves as observers, but it was we who observed and bitterly mocked their celebrations of life.

Our shells of staleness proved deceitful. They cracked, making us bleed even more—we felt lonely while mocking. We were left in the catastrophe with a parcel of aid thrown from afar, and so we learned to count on ourselves, being stronger than even our strengths. The unfamiliar feeling of metal inside—is it the steel?—first appeared in late February and has returned often since. If ours, metal was our friend. It protected us on the battlefields and in our homes when missiles were launched, and the steel feeling inside dried our tears and called for action. We were different again now: fiercer and stronger. We learned to plan, calculate, and prioritize, and thus returned to the basics while leaving aside whatever seemed unnecessary. Metal made us exhausted to the utmost limit and yet we still demanded more—imagine trying to cover a wound with metal. But you need metal to fix a broken bone and metal to heal a broken human.

Yet even rods cannot endure pressure forever when separate from one another. Our speech became societal, grounded in common grief and mutual support, and so we casually responded to "How are you?" with frontline updates or the number of killed and injured in the last missile attack. Every conversation was one about our guys in the trenches, about civilians in our cities, about our children in captivity, about our prisoners of war, about our dead. Sometimes, "I" or "we" could not understand where "we" ends and "I" begins.

—You know, I noticed that when I talk to the surgeons or the military by phone, my voice goes several tones down.

My sister laughs in the middle of the room. She might sound young and cheerful but can converse in sharp sentences braced with military and medical jargon. She is a volunteer whose ability to handle complex requests can be questioned in the male-dominated field of military medicine. She lowers her voice while speaking to indicate her confidence and knowledge. The next time I listen to her, I notice her voice going down again and again, whether she is speaking with a chaplain, a surgeon, or a chief medical officer.

—What did we talk about before the war? my sister asks me.

We cannot remember. No one can.

The transformation of our speech remains alien to our lives, just like the war itself. We expect that the invaders will finally leave, and, in an instant, there will be no need for the war language, and gradually, we might even forget it. But what if it remains forever? I fear that my sister's voice will never return and that all these words imbued with wartime meanings will never return to the peaceful ones. Will we ever laugh at something other than macabre, wartime life and death? Will we ever talk without interlacing every topic with our sorrow? Will our language ever become "normal?" We don't know what the new norm would be and cannot guess how we might help or hurt each other in our changing innerness.

Speech is a mirror that reflects transformations that occur so deep that we hardly notice them otherwise. We are divided inside so that our kaleidoscopic life is now reduced to black and white, to contradictory feelings and meanings—just as the war is. And nonetheless, are we sure that anything new has arisen in us? Before the war—if we try to remember anything from that time—we bore similar intentions and feelings inside. The war brought them to the surface, magnified them, and polished them. It might be that everything "new" we notice has always been present. It might be that the war is a magnifying glass held above the inner self—we now clearly see who we are.

к== ковані вогнем і залізом
інфопросторами і болем
зрештою, всі ми ставали іншими
залишаючись насправді тими
ким були від самісінького початку[16]

Wartime Glossary

War language is not bound to military jargon. It seeps into our everyday language, turning it upside down. Traditional glossaries usually provide a list of fixed meanings. However, war switches their order, and the new ones reflect unstable associations, the changing manner of speech, and new modes of understanding. Peacetime words are now imbued with wartime, metallic, life-or-death meanings—words are mobilized, riddled with nuances and feelings that none of the existing dictionaries can capture.

Тривога (alarm) became a common denominator for both anxiety and air raid sirens.

Інфраструктура (infrastructure) evokes a feeling of weakness and reminds us of destruction, ruin, and fire; it also refers to constant danger, to something that needs protection. It addresses people working to renovate the systems after every strike—it stands for admiration of their work.

Дрони (drones) do not capture beautiful scenery; they take off, chase, pursue, hit, explode, and kill.

Ракети (rockets) are no longer about airspace technologies but about missiles, death, and destruction.

Обмін (exchange) is no longer monetary or financial; it is the last hope of thousands of people whose loved ones are prisoners of war. But why do we exchange human bodies or human souls?

Переговори (negotiations) became a scary word; it means that some outsiders ignorantly want you to surrender and suffer occupation just to comfort themselves and remove your bothersome presence from their life. It means a superficial understanding of history, modern-day situations, your losses, or any of the context; with it, you are not wanted or not worth listening to.

Зерно (grain) is more about power games and less about the fields.

Тортури (torture) transcends the chronology of the Middle Ages.

Посадка (planting) and *зеленка* (brilliant green) do not refer to vegetables or medicine for minor injuries. Both now signify frontline demarcations, half-destroyed trees, and scarce but life-saving greenery. They mean attack, assault, holding the line, hiding in disguise, and constantly being aware of the danger.

Турнікет (turnstiles) no longer stand at the metro entrance or the university reception. The word has almost lost its peaceful light metallic or orange color; it is now black, related to blood and mortal inquiry: tourniquet.

Even **кров** (blood) has lost its original meaning and connotations. It is no longer associated with Grandma's blood pressure, with menstrual blood, or blood at a crime scene in a detective series; it recalls vivid pictures from the stretchers and parts of one's body; it accumulates in the asphalt holes after another missile attack on civilians; it is packed, transferred to trenches, and transfused there via IV lines; thus, blood is something in permanent shortage. "Your blood can fight," states the donation center's slogan. The blood cannot flow peacefully anymore; even blood has to fight. And it can: pictures of empty blood bags posted by paramedics mean saved lives and invite real action and support for the front line. Ukrainians' blood narrative is a part of the steel inside our backbone, protecting and inspiring us. Isn't it strange that blood has a metallic taste and is full of metal as well?

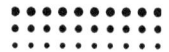

15

Should Have Known

DIÁNA VONNÁK

When the Polish anthropologist Bronisław Malinowski arrived in the Trobriand Islands in 1915, he was an Austro-Hungarian subject in a British territory at risk of internment. Stranded there, he stayed put and turned this long-term presence into the instrument that defines social anthropology even today. But World War I was not the only war that shaped his work in a profound manner: from archaeological work coming out recently we know that the kula, the intricate ceremonial exchange system he described as proof of the universality of rational human thought, was in fact a colonial phenomenon, the result of a decades-long pacification process.

In recent years, this story has gained a new twist for me. Anthropology has come a long way from what it was in that explicitly colonial context, when it mostly engaged with communities far from metropolitan centers. Distance itself, whether geographic, class-based, or epistemic, has been problematized in myriad ways. But there is something in the position of the contemporary observer whose craft is based on linking quotidian, modest scales of observation to large-scale processes. Geopolitics can feel like the background against which our work unfolds; we use it crudely and take some of it for granted. But the past few years taught me that scales collapse in certain places and times, and you might find yourself playing the role of a witness.

I grew up in Budapest, but as an anthropologist, I came of age in Ukraine during the Donbas war. As I was developing the proposal my PhD research would be based on, protesters gathered on the Maidan. By the time I got news that I had secured the funding, an unnamed war broke out. I arrived in Lviv in West Ukraine in 2015, a few months after the second Minsk agreement froze the front lines. I wanted to study the collapse of the USSR and the subsequent political and economic transformation through the lens of debates around heritage and urban governance. Lviv was 1,200 kilometers from Sloviansk where Igor Girkin, the military spin doctor and veteran of wars in Transnistria and Chechnya, first led militants to storm the city council on April 12, 2014.

Russian surface-to-air missiles, shady local business schemers becoming heads of puppet republics, a mixture of thugs and "political technologists" spinning wheels from Crimea to Kramatorsk, paid protesters, real protesters—the undeclared Donbas war was disorienting from afar. In Lviv, I found myself seeking out the internally displaced, interviewing elderly residents of a care home, students from Eastern Ukraine, and veterans. My research assistant, a Luhansk native, recounted arduous and costly visits home through checkpoints whenever he visited his grandmother. Friends went to fight and returned. They spoke little of what happened. Later, I spent time in Kramatorsk with a friend who worked for the Organization for Security and Co-operation in Europe (OSCE) monitoring mission and caught a glimpse of her burnout over the quality of the work they were able to provide.

These were pieces in an enormous puzzle at the fringes of my vision, something I sought out between ethnographic and archival work enmeshed in the local politics of Lviv. I had no better explanation for doing this than a gut feeling that this war was lurking in my ostensibly far-removed research world. But people's biographies led directly to the front. The distance between the Donbas and Lviv is nothing once you consider the two million displaced and hundreds of thousands of soldiers who would serve there before February 2022. The war radiated across the social fabric, regardless of the confusion and the lack of will or interest to see it, despite all the misinformation and prejudices.

Looking back on it all, the escalation seems like a straight line leading to only one future: the one we are living in right now. It is a striking, slow geopolitical unraveling, the end of the post–Cold War status quo. It feels absurd not to have anticipated it with high confidence. This, of course, is an illusion, and one that tells us a lot about the extent to which the present moment retrospectively orders our attention, wading through unmetabolized experience and a cacophony of guesswork, motivated speech, misinformation, and rudimentary analysis. We could call it a fog of war in the epistemic sense, but if we flip this around, this fog is ever-present, the stuff of fieldwork, and navigating it is a predicament of any contemporaneous empirical research.

On paper, ethnography should be an exercise in radical openness. We are trained to let go of plans, to readjust and make space for the unexpected; we should be ready to shift focus when we notice that our assumptions have led us astray. But assumptions and patterns of attention are not that easy to catch—and here I am reminded of Malinowski again, the stranded contemporary, the enemy alien seeking order amid chaotic wartime change, unintentionally contraposing equilibrium to people with whom he worked, while his own world was on fire. When working in volatile contexts, facing something unprecedented, it is all too easy to look without realizing what you are looking at, lacking the political imagination and experience to prevent yourself from falling prey to wishful thinking, unprepared to read the signs. It is difficult even to select which signs to pay attention to in the first place.

I spent the last few months before the full-scale invasion in Kyiv. Life there felt like a pendulum swinging us between spikes of anxiety and a defiant, hedonistic carelessness. As foreign friends were leaving, veteran acquaintances quietly prepared for the worst, and many in our circles opined that the US warnings were moves in a geopolitical game. The only way to orient ourselves would have been to systematically review intelligence reports, military analyses, and diplomatic communiqués; then cut through clutter and compare evidence. This is a disorienting, highly technical exercise, a full-time job if you want to take it seriously. Most of us lacked the specific literacy anyway. Crucially, most of us also lacked the knowledge of what war-in-the-making could look like. The future felt half-open, ominous.

I work with questions that used to have little to do with grand strategy or military maneuvers. In those months of tense limbo in Kyiv, I often came close to expecting a serious escalation, war spilling over from the Donbas, but even with hundreds of thousands of troops crowding the border, I never thought it would happen the way it eventually did. Arguably, my shock could be excused. But it felt like a professional failure anyway. This new reality radically altered the decade I lived through, changing what were meaningful signs and premonitions, calling into question patterns of common misinterpretation and ultimately raising concerns about the politics of these shortcomings.

My dilemmas about the limitations of ethnography and my own limitations were not about the fact of the invasion, per se. Instead, I felt the full-scale war exposed the frailties of witnessing and observing, of the epistemic challenges of contemporaneity. I spent the past winter piecing together microhistories of single days, asking myself what I could have known, comparing it with the diary entries and field notes I took, staring at the gap between what turned out to be crucial and what I paid attention to—the places where my interests, assumptions led me astray. This is not an exercise in self-blame. Rather, it is a fraught attempt to learn something about the twin predicaments of living through and making sense of the war.

It was those intense months of limbo that prompted me to review my memories and material from the Donbas in a systematic fashion for the first time. Likewise, after February 2022, decade-old conversations with Indian soldiers in my first fieldwork or scenes from my prolonged stays in Israel and Lebanon would suddenly emerge in my mind, making sense in a new way. With my recently acquired literacy of societies at war, I wonder how certain details had not stood out to me when I encountered them, whether in East Jerusalem in 2012 or in Kramatorsk in 2016. Through these loops, these systematic reviews, it became easier to trace the outlines of how accumulated experiences fed back to who I am as an observer.

To work in this world, where our political imagination and experiential base are far outpaced by the events around us, I find I must be a bit like Baron Munchausen who pulled himself out of the puddle by his own hair. It takes serious epistemic work to identify where it is that you are a reasonably equipped witness-observer, where your training, politics, and past experience might be an ally, and when you need to actively work against them. This has stakes everywhere, anytime. But in wartime, allowing the world to shatter what you thought were solid foundations seems the only intellectually honest way to both observe and participate.

16

Your Understanding Is Not Enough

SASHA KOROBEINIKOV

In early August 2015, the Department of History at Central European University in Budapest organized a conference for undergraduate students titled "Empire and Nation." Many students from various countries, including Ukraine, attended the conference. At the time, it had been more than a year since Russia's annexation of Crimea and the beginning of its military occupation of the Donetsk and Luhansk regions. During the general sessions and receptions, Ukrainian students tried their best to draw attention to these recent events and the potential for a "big war" in Ukraine, as we referred to it back then. Unfortunately, most participants chose to ignore these concerns. Those who did pay attention joked about the "excessively nervous tension" among these students and advised them to "go smoke weed" instead.

Ironically, at the end of the event, only students from Ukraine, Belarus, and the Russian Federation, including myself, remained in the reception hall. We had long discussions about the ongoing war and its impact on the daily lives of people in the occupied territories. We considered the likelihood of a large-scale Russian invasion of Ukraine and speculated about the possible role of Belarus in it. Despite the emotional discomfort they caused, these conversations ultimately fostered a common understanding and strengthened bonds between students from countries already at war. The Ukrainian students expressed frustration at their unsuccessful efforts to be heard by the international student community, whose indifference was likely due to a lack of familiarity with the situation in Ukraine and an inability to perceive the catastrophic nature of the unfolding events. They were all more than eager to speak, to be heard, and to be understood, as they repeatedly warned that Russia's ambitions were not limited to Crimea and could extend further.

Being heard and understood presumes that the listener is not only ready to listen to your words but also able to comprehend their essence and grasp their meaning. Achieving this comprehension has become even more complex in today's wartime conditions, where the political construction of an enemy, defined by its radical otherness, dehumanizes it. This dehumanization, in turn, justifies the continuation of the conflict by framing it in terms of moral or existential dichotomies. Misunderstandings between the conflicting sides, fueled by these dichotomies and negative portrayals, are often exacerbated and create barriers that are difficult to overcome. Russian propaganda and cultural stereotypes about Ukrainians extend well beyond the start of the war in 2014. Narratives of Ukrainian otherness—such as the "backwardness of Ukrainian culture," the "rustic language," or the "nationalistic character of Ukrainians"—have been actively circulated in the Russian media and press, especially since the collapse of the USSR and the emergence of the independent Russian Federation, and have only intensified in recent years, preparing the ground for the widespread support among Russia's masses for an invasion. Since 2014, and especially since 2022, the Ukrainian media's portrayal of the enemy has significantly shaped the perceptions of the Russian population. In response to Russian aggression, these media outlets have intensified antagonism by demonizing the entire Russian population, thereby deepening existing animosities. This makes me wonder if understanding on a human level is still possible.

Understanding also means taking the perspective of others and sensing their needs and desires. It is about having a clear vision of how to help without inflicting harm. In the context of war, this alignment and vision require overcoming inner barriers and fostering new layers of affective bonds. The Russo–Ukrainian war has created a profound shift and a paradox. Despite the political and military support of Ukraine's allies, achieving mutual understanding on a personal level remains exceptionally challenging. This difficulty persists irrespective of the increased global awareness of Ukraine.

For those outside of war zones, listening to witnesses and participants is much easier than understanding their logic. Many who do not have traumatic war experiences deliberately distance themselves, whether out of reluctance to engage with personal stories, fear of making mistakes, or sheer lack of context. Take Germany, for example, a country that has welcomed a significant number of Ukrainians since 2022 and has also become a permanent home for me. Here, Ukrainians often struggle to find common ground with locals. The barriers are not primarily linguistic or cultural. Frequently, with genuine intentions to display openness and inquire about the well-being of someone from Ukraine, Germans ask the seemingly harmless question, "Are you okay?" This question can inadvertently irritate Ukrainians, for whom it is obvious that they are not okay in the aftermath of the full-scale Russian invasion, and who may be expecting a simpler question: "How are you feeling?" In addition, the ubiquity of Russian propaganda and soft power in Europe adds another layer of difficulty. Comments that blur the lines between Russians and Ukrainians, such as telling a Ukrainian woman on a train from Leipzig to Budapest that she has "very deep Russian eyes" or indifferently shelving Ukrainian authors in the Russian Literature section of European bookstores, can be upsetting. Like most of Western Europe, today's Germany highlights the stark contrast between life during wartime and the relative peace enjoyed by those without traumatic experiences. Trauma is a deeply distressing and disruptive state that overwhelms an individual's ability to cope. It develops into a possibly endless cycle of suffering, especially when coupled with interactions that signal a lack of awareness. Indeed, war trauma creates an additional barrier to the complex and fragile process of mutual understanding.

The 2015 conference was my first opportunity to communicate with students from Ukraine, with whom I found many commonalities despite the political and military contradictions and constructed otherness. What we shared included the experience of growing up in the post-Soviet space with its political and economic fluctuations, the oppressive physical environment, and knowing what it means to lose loved ones and be without a home. I was surprised at how easy it was for me, someone who had lost both parents before entering university and whose home no longer existed, to talk about trauma with people who had experienced the shock of the annexation of Crimea and the start of the war. Despite my efforts to avoid discussing my intimate biographical details, I believe that the Ukrainian students could detect the undertones of traumatic experience in my remarks. This unique background allowed me not only to overcome the fear of a possible aggressive reaction from the other and to begin to communicate with the Ukrainian students at the conference but also to recognize them as people who needed something very particular—to be heard and understood.

After two years of holding weekly mentoring sessions with IUFU students, I am no longer convinced that experiencing trauma or growing up in a post-Soviet environment is a necessary precondition of understanding, although these factors may have, to a large extent, facilitated our interactions. Nor am I convinced that understanding requires deep historical knowledge of Russian colonialism and human agency in imperial contexts, the subjects of my professional expertise. What I am certain of, however, is that if we have a genuine intention to help and not just to *display openness or inquire about the well-being of someone from Ukraine*, one way to do so is to support independent educational initiatives that focus on empowering Ukrainian students and laying the groundwork for a delicate yet possible mutual understanding.

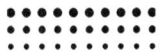

17

Vulnerability and Resilience

NADIIA CHERVINSKA

The tradition of the oppressed teaches us that the "state of emergency" in which we live is not the exception but the rule.

—W. Benjamin, "Theses on the Philosophy of History," 1940

"Be brave like Ukraine" is a slogan often used in support of the Ukrainian war effort. I see it everywhere—on the billboards on my way home, stickers on my classmates' phones, and the Facebook covers of my long-distance relatives. It is meant to embody the resilience of Ukrainian society, showing the values we choose to praise—strength, toughness, and self-sufficiency. These values seem necessary when your country is under constant attack. Yet, the pervasiveness of this message is overwhelming. I feel constantly pushed to live up to it. Any other form of self-expression that might expose my weakness, either physical or mental, feels shameful: I want to hide, overcome, and avoid them at all costs. "Be brave like Ukraine," becomes, "Be brave like every Ukrainian."

I do not question the slogan; I comply with it. I accept that performing strength is a part of being Ukrainian—it does not matter whether it is the strength I show or I truly have. Admitting my weakness is almost like admitting defeat. Yet, no matter how much I try to protect myself, I will never be completely safe. Like everyone else, I have breaking points both physical and mental. It is exactly because invulnerability is impossible that I strive for it so much. I want to pretend that I am not affected by the war, that I never felt the pain of losing a friend, that I never wondered if my loved ones are safe, that I never doubted that I would wake up next morning. I want to think that my life has stayed the same, that I am untouched by the horrors around me. Acting like I am unaffected helps me keep going and function in daily life—it is a way to adjust to the new realities of war at my own pace. I find in it a form of resistance, a refusal to let the enemy control my own life. When I receive an air-raid alarm notification, I do not go to hide in a shelter—I go to the nearest coffee shop for a V-60 and drink it to the sounds of the explosions in the air. When there is no electricity, I open my laptop and connect to the power generator to submit my work on time. I have not slept properly for weeks but I try to meet the deadlines. When I see in the news that a Russian missile hit another residential building, I make a repost and go to my class because I have to present a paper and cannot afford to grieve.

I easily embrace the narratives that idealize bravery. They comfort me, reassure me, and give me some stability. They convince me that "герої не вмирають" ("Heroes do not die"). Everyone keeps repeating this message along with stories of their bravery. They are supposed to unify us with a standard of strength to aim for. These narratives worked in the short term but have become problematic in the long run. Thinking that I can always perform strength goes against my ability to be affected and my dependence on others—something inherently embedded in the human condition. The efforts to hide my vulnerability eventually become just as dehumanizing as war itself. Trying to stay unaffected has led me to isolation: in trying to protect myself from experiencing fear, pain, and loss, I also distance myself from empathy, compassion, and hope. I no longer know how to respond to the experiences of those around me, especially when they are different from what I have been through. This is where all my indifference and insensitivity come from—I got used to suffering in silence. I do not seek support, and I deny others a chance to offer or ask for it.

I feel powerless. I cannot change the realities of the war, so I just choose to pretend these realities have not changed me. Yet, my life has fundamentally changed in ways I cannot ignore anymore. What seemed normal for me is no longer the same. I will never be able to go back to "before the war"—and "after the war" may never happen. The state of emergency is not just governmental policy anymore—it is my new mode of living. I carry a tourniquet with me all the time like a new accessory. I plan when to sleep, when to shower, and even when to use the elevator. I have a plan on what to do in case of being attacked by nuclear missiles. I have tried hard to normalize things that are not normal. To move beyond this state, I need to accept how the war has changed me and my sense of self. I need to recognize the new reality—only then it will be possible to recover my experiences and reclaim control over my life. I need to embrace the pain, fear, and loss rather than resist them. I need to accept that heroes do, indeed, die, and that the pain of loss makes me doubt whether their deaths were worth the sacrifice. Only then will I understand what is really at stake.

When I acknowledge my own suffering, it grounds me in reality because I must confront my fragility, accept my limitations, and move forward despite them. I recognize that a common experience of suffering, grief, and mourning unifies me with others. We all keep on proving our bravery by living under wartime conditions and not surrendering to the enemy. Acknowledging vulnerability will not negate it because it will not make us weak: not on a personal level, and not as a community. Acknowledging vulnerability can thus turn into a source of strength, embedded not only in personal responses. It can help us shape collective action, ethical rules, and social norms. It can help us rethink the way we treat others, offering solidarity and support. It can help us question the values we prioritize and whether they protect and help others the way we would like them to protect and help us. It can also help us prevent others from going through the same pain. Even if it will not change the course of the war, it can certainly shape how we experience it and how we will recover from it.

18

Inheriting Destruction

NATALIIA SHULIAKOVA

What is presented to us is an object—home. We want to see our grandmother washing dishes in the corner of the kitchen. Instead, we observe a double exposure: the clinking of dishes surfaces from recent memory while looking at a single object left in our grandmother's kitchen—the sink, without running water.

We, people who lost our homes, hold on to the home that exists in our minds. The object—home—begins to fade into the past, slips into memories, and becomes blurred. To see it again is to see it as a new object, a replacement of the previous one. It has lived in our memory in bits and pieces, constantly drifting away but never getting closer to us. We hold on to the images of tapestries on the walls, inscriptions on the staircase, and Grandma washing dishes. When we notice the sink buried in bare cement all around the fifteen-yard kitchen floor, we become acutely aware of the substitution made in our absence. With increased sensitivity not only to the feeling of loss but also of home, we are exposed simultaneously to love, grief, pain, self-pity, and pity for the space itself.

Level zero: Everything is leveled to the ground

Immediate destruction

We are tempted to think that all is gone when forests are scorched, bridges blown up, houses shelled, and all that is left are bare sinks in the same places they used to be, the money tree plant from the windowsill now smeared on the ceiling, and naked walls. We then witness ruins that lie before our eyes or take center stage in news coverage through a 50 mm camera lens. We did not even have time to turn around to remember home the way it was before; we later recognized it in reportage. We know which part of the house took the hit, we learned the exact time of the missile launch, and we know when our personal territory shrank. We are aware of the facts and dates. We have seen the city captured after it was burned to the ground. We may sympathize with the home's debris and the pain that its existence presents. On level zero, we think that all is gone. But nothing is ever truly gone. It is taken, rearranged, and discarded in a burlap sack by state emergency services. What did not fit in the sackcloth—unwanted memories, nightly clattering of dishes, father's honorary place at the kitchen table—finds a place in our memory and travels wherever we go until we reach level one.

Level one: The mastery of designation

Mediated destruction

The destruction is both instantaneous and prolonged, while the moment of physical damage is quick and definite. What happens next? The burned tapestry slides down the wall to the dustbin, the snoring neighbor from downstairs moves to the IDP center, and tattered wallpaper reveals inscriptions on the walls written during the first move-in. Those stretched-in-time changes that others exercise over the space that we own(ed) are done in our absence. We do not live through those transformations of our cities, do not control them, but only spy on homes that change faster than we can follow.

They say that everything comes back at the sensory level of familiar surfaces. As I walked around the half-ruined house, I had to refer to the pictures in my memory constantly: we were a "big family," and I was scared of darkness and our long corridor with a light switch at its end. Now, walking down the same hallway, it no longer seems long and scary—it is defenseless and bare, and the echoing footsteps on the cement floor expose the reverberating sounds present there before. The workers who tore off the laminate flooring and rearranged the careful structure of the library into one massive burlap sack of books were not the ones destroying the territory, but they were the ones intruding on it. We seem doomed to never feel entirely at home unless we are living in our bygone image of it. We bring the baggage of home fragments to new cities, and the idea of returning to the real home, the one taken by a predatory act of war, makes everywhere feel unsafe. The return phase comes differently, but level two engulfs us when we dare to return, assuming it is possible.

Level two: Return to the doorsteps

Inheriting destruction(s)

Time has frozen in these walls. It has been covered with cracks that are now filled with plaster. Here, returning home means being faced with a ghost town, unable to process, accept, and eventually be present in the place as it is now. The neighborhood reminds us of people who no longer exist, who have left, who have changed, who have been killed. Graffiti made during high school remind us of better times, loud tourists, and rain-soaked abandoned towns whose residents left behind most of their personal belongings.

We cannot fathom the immense loss of the city we have formed with our gaze, and the best we can do is carve our name on the newly plastered walls to render our existence. While away from home, we can still carry its image. Once we return, we must admit that the home we've carried with us is no longer there—"the dead tree gives no shelter." The city has turned into a monument of itself. Returning to it would be falling for a ruse, an unconscious act of self-deception, like believing in the power of all words starting with re- and de-: deoccupy, regain, rebuild, reappropriate. We never return to our childhood homes with Dad's music blasting from his loudspeaker, nor regain the territories with the same city plan and beachfront without excavated trenches, and nor can we re-own the sea without newly established signs that warn us about the underwater mines. The claim of ownership has to be assigned from scratch, over and over again. We will have to find the courage to reclaim the place: the house that shattered into black snowflakes overnight, the forest plantation that now holds hundreds of unfulfilled promises, and the overgrown pathways that will never conform to their earlier footprints. People who have lost their homes will first have to find a heart to reclaim its ruins—ruins that we did not create but now have to love.

Notes

The authors of this introduction as well as all the contributors to the volume would like to express their gratitude to Sarah Cypher for her incredible care and empathy with editing the manuscript, to Mark Baker for his dedicated and attentive language editing, as well as to Christopher Beem, Jan Kubik, Xymena Kurowska, Marina Simakova, and Renáta Uitz for commenting on our drafts.

1 Hannah Arendt, "The Crisis in Education," chap. 5 in *Between Past and Future: Six Exercises in Political Thought* (New York: The Viking Press, 1961), 174.

2 On the campaign against CEU, see Zsolt Enyedi, "The Central European University in the Trenches," in *Brave New Hungary: Mapping the "System of National Cooperation,"* ed. János M. Kovács and Balázs Trencsényi (Lanham, MD: Lexington Books, 2020), 243–66.

3 Bertolt Brecht, "On the Formalistic Character of the Theory of Realism," in Theodor Adorno, Walter Benjamin, Ernst Bloch, Bertolt Brecht, and Georg Lukacs, *Aesthetics and Politics*, ed. Fredric Jameson (London: Verso Books, 2007), 74.

4 The images of suffering subjects. Oraib Toukan, "Cruel Images," *e-flux* 96 (2019).

5 Susan Sontag, *Regarding the Pain of Others* (New York: Picador, 2003), 24.

6 Roland Barthes, *A Lover's Discourse: Fragments* (New York: Hill & Wang, 2001), 57.

7 Interview with Lisa Bukreyeva for the *Ukrainian Warchive Project*. In the interview, Lisa mentions that having changed her IP address, she could not see any of the war-related hashtags actively circulated by the Ukrainian users.

8 Francesco Faeta, "War, Constructions of National Identity, and Photography," *Rivista di Studi di Fotografia* no. 4 (2016): 18.

9 "Freedom of Speech," accessed June 22, 2024, https://compliance.admin.ox.ac.uk/freedom-of-speech.

10 Czesław Miłosz, "Campo dei Fiori," 1943, Warsaw, https://www.poetryfoundation.org/poems/49751/campo-dei-fiori.

11 Jorge Luis Borges, "Mirrors," https://ronnowpoetry.com/contents/borges/Mirrors.html.

12 In this essay, all dated quotations of this type can be found in "The Diary of a Ukrainian Soldier," trans. Jason Cieply, https://zona.media/article/2022/10/30/wardiary.

13 Project *Dnevniki 22*, October 5, 2022, Statya Voloshyna, Odesa, https://t.me/dnevniki_22/629.

14 Stanislav Vasin, "Homo Donbassus, or What the War Changed," https://zn.ua/ukr/internal/homo-donbassus-abo-scho-zminila-viyna-_.html.

15 *Brigade, pocket* (an encirclement of military forces), *cyborgs* (nickname for Ukrainian troops who defended Donetsk International Airport from May 26, 2014, to January 22, 2015), *front, wounded, killed in action.*

16 forged with fire and metal

   infospaces and pain

   ultimately, we all were becoming different

   while remaining, in fact, the same

   who we were

   from the very beginning

                              (translated by Tetiana Zemliakova)

IUFU Courses and Course Directors, 2022–2024

Spring Semester 2022

- **Symbolic Geography, Contested Identities, and Mass Violence: Ukrainian History in European Contexts**. Course director: Vladimir Petrović (Central European University Democracy Institute / Institute for Contemporary History, Belgrade)
- **Culture and Heritage Studies.** Course codirectors: Volodymyr Kulikov (Ukrainian Catholic University, Lviv) and Dóra Mérai (Central European University)
- **Between Norms and Realities: Challenges to Europeanization, Democratization, and the Rule of Law in a Transnational Context.** Course codirectors: Oleksiy Kononov (CEU Democracy Institute), Nazarii Stetsyk (Ivan Franko National University, Lviv), and Renáta

Uitz (Central European University / CEU Democracy Institute)

- **Transformation, Conflict, and Migration: Study of Exceptions from Rules, Vulnerability to Risks, and Unacceptable Conditions.** Course codirectors: Volodymyr Artiukh (University of Oxford), and Tatyjana Szafonova (Comenius University, Bratislava)

Fall Semester 2022

- **Ukraine: Imperial, Soviet, Independent, European.** Course codirectors: Nazarii Stetsyk (Ivan Franko National University, Lviv) and Vladimir Petrović (Central European University Democracy Institute / Institute for Contemporary History, Belgrade)
- **History of the Public Sphere in Ukraine and East Central Europe.** Course director: Ostap Sereda (Central European University / Ukrainian Catholic University, Lviv / Imre Kertész Kolleg, Jena)
- **War, Memory, and the City. Shaping Collective Remembrance and Re-Articulation of Past in Ukraine in European Contexts.** Course director: Tetiana Vodotyka (Institute of History of Ukraine, NASU, Kyiv / Georg-August-Universität, Göttingen)
- **Migration, Displacement and (Trans)National Solidarities in Ukraine in the Global Contexts.** Course

director: Viktoriya Sereda (Institute of Ethnology, NASU, Lviv / Ukrainian Catholic University, Lviv / Forum Transregionale Studien, Berlin)

- **Heritage-Based Post-War Urban Reconstruction in Ukraine.** Course codirectors: Volodymyr Kulikov (Ukrainian Catholic University, Lviv / University of Texas at Austin), Dóra Mérai (Central European University), and Loes Veldpaus (Newcastle University)
- **Ukraine in/and Europe: Frameworks of European Integration.** Course codirectors: Maryna Rabinovych (University of Agder) and Marta Mochulska (Ivan Franko National University, Lviv)
- **Ideologies on the Move: Transnational Ideas in Local Intellectual Cultures.** Course director: Tetiana Zemliakova (European University Institute, Florence)

Spring Semester 2023

- **Rethinking Ukrainian Studies in a Global Context.** Course codirectors: Ostap Sereda (Central European University / Ukrainian Catholic University, Lviv / Imre Kertész Kolleg, Jena) and Balázs Trencsényi (Central European University)
- **Public History.** Course codirectors: Viktoriya Sereda (Institute of Ethnology, NASU, Lviv / Ukrainian Catholic University, Lviv / Forum Transregionale Studien, Berlin)

and Bohdan Shumylovych (Ukrainian Catholic University, Lviv / Center for Urban History, Lviv)

- **Re-interpreting European Security in the Aftermath of Russia's War in Ukraine.** Course codirectors: Thomas Fetzer (Central European University), Xymena Kurowska (Central European University), Maksym Yakovlyev (National University of Kyiv-Mohyla Academy), and Kateryna Zarembo (Technical University, Darmstadt)

- **Rule of Law and Human Rights: Old Challenges and New Opportunities in Times of War and Uncertainty.** Course codirectors: Nazarii Stetsyk (Ivan Franko National University, Lviv / Kellogg Institute for International Studies, University of Notre Dame), and Dmytro Vovk (Yaroslav the Wise National Law University, Kharkiv)

- **Social Entrepreneurship: Emergence, Models, and Impact.** Course codirectors: Volodymyr Kulikov (Ukrainian Catholic University / University of Texas at Austin), Dóra Mérai (Central European University), and Tetiana Vodotyka (Institute of History of Ukraine, NASU, Kyiv / Georg-August-Universität Göttingen)

- **War and Media.** Course codirectors: Taras Fedirko (University of Glasgow) and Oksana Sarkisova (Central European University / Vera and Donald Blinken Open Society Archives, Budapest)

- **(Post)conflict Transformations in the Western Balkans: Drawing Insights for Ukraine?** Course director: Vladimir Petrović (Central European University / CEU Democracy Institute / Institute for Contemporary History, Belgrade)
- **Graduate Masterclass on Entering Global Academia.** Course director: Alexandra Vacroux (Davis Center at Harvard University)

Fall Semester, 2023

- **Imagined Geography of Ukraine from the Late Eighteenth till the Late Twentieth Centuries: Regions, Cities, Landscapes, Population.** Course codirectors: Kateryna Dysa (National University of Kyiv-Mohyla Academy / University of Oxford) and Martin-Oleksandr Kisly (National University of Kyiv-Mohyla Academy)
- **Late Soviet and Post-Soviet Counter-Cultures in Ukraine and East Central Europe.** Course codirectors: Bohdan Shumylovych (Ukrainian Catholic University, Lviv / Center for Urban History, Lviv) and Balázs Trencsényi (Central European University / CEU Institute for Advanced Study)
- **Ukraine's EU Integration: Compliance and Resilience in Times of War and Geopolitical Rivalries.** Course codirectors: Inna Melnykovska (Central European University) and Nazarii Stetsyk (Ivan Franko National University,

Lviv / Kellogg Institute for International Studies, University of Notre Dame)

- **Sexuality and Decoloniality.** Course codirectors: Nadiya Chushak (National University of Kyiv-Mohyla Academy / Bard College Berlin), Maria Mayerchyk (Institute of Ethnology, NASU, Lviv / University of Greifswald), and Olga Plakhotnik (University of Greifswald)
- **Identities-Borders-Orders: Migration and Belonging.** Course codirectors: Oksana Mikheieva (Ukrainian Catholic University, Lviv / European University Viadrina, Frankfurt an der Oder) and Viktoriya Sereda (Institute of Ethnology, NASU, Lviv / Ukrainian Catholic University, Lviv / Wissenschaftskolleg zu Berlin)
- **The Politics of Warfare: Key Concepts in the History of Modern Military Thought.** Course director: Tetiana Zemliakova (European University Institute, Florence)
- **Western Balkans: Imperial Legacies, Nation-Building, State Disintegration.** Course codirectors: Vladimir Petrović (Central European University / CEU Democracy Institute / Institute for Contemporary History, Belgrade) and Aleksandar Pavlović (University of Belgrade)

Spring Semester, 2024

- **Intellectual Debates in Modern Ukrainian History and Contemporary Public Sphere.** Course codirectors: Ostap Sereda (Central European University / Ukrainian

Catholic University, Lviv / Bard College Berlin) and Balázs Trencsényi (Central European University / CEU Institute for Advanced Study)

- **Rethinking Nationalism: Conceptual Frameworks and Political Challenges.** Course codirectors: Valeria Korablyova (Charles University, Prague) and Vladimir Petrović (Central European University / CEU Democracy Institute / Institute for Contemporary History in Belgrade)

- **Sustaining Rule of Law and Democracy in Ukraine amidst War and Post-War Reconstruction.** Course codirectors: Olena Boryslavska (Ivan Franko National University, Lviv) and Nazarii Stetsyk (Ivan Franko National University, Lviv / Kellogg Institute for International Studies, University of Notre Dame)

- **Cultural Diplomacy during the War: Practices and Institutional Strategies.** Course director: Yana Barinova (ERSTE Foundation, Vienna)

- **European Union Enlargement and Reform: A Common Path for Ukraine's European Future.** Course codirectors: Veronica Anghel (European University Institute, Florence) and Inna Melnykovska (Central European University)

- **Beyond War and Peace: Rethinking the Balkans for Ukraine.** Course codirectors: Aleksandar Pavlović (University of Belgrade) and Olesia Marković (National University of Kyiv-Mohyla Academy).

Fall Semester, 2024

- **(Re)thinking "Soviet": Modern Ukrainian Identity and the Legacy of Communism.** Course director: Olena Palko (University of Basel)
- **Civil Society and the State in Ukraine.** Course codirectors: Diána Vonnák (University of Stirling) and Taras Fedirko (University of Glasgow)
- **The Security and Political Economy of EU Integration: Theory and Policy.** Course codirectors: Veronica Anghel (European University Institute, Florence) and Inna Melnykovska (Central European University)
- **War, Peace, and the Politics of Uncertainty.** Course codirectors: Tetiana Zemliakova (CEU Democracy Institute) and Guillaume Lancereau (European University Institute, Florence)
- **Sexuality and Decoloniality.** Course codirectors: Nadiya Chushak (National University of Kyiv-Mohyla Academy / Bard College Berlin) and Olena Dmytryk (University of Cambridge)
- **Migration, Belonging, Policies.** Course codirectors: Oksana Mikheieva (ZOIS, Berlin / Ukrainian Catholic University, Lviv / European University Viadrina, Frankfurt an der Oder) and Viktoriya Sereda (Institute of Ethnology, NASU, Lviv / Ukrainian Catholic University, Lviv / Wissenschaftskolleg zu Berlin)

- **Politics and Narratives at European Borderlands: Rethinking Balkans for Ukraine.** Course codirectors: Marija Mandić (University of Belgrade), Olesia Marković (National University of Kyiv-Mohyla Academy), and Aleksandar Pavlović (University of Belgrade)
- **Research Methods for the Social Sciences.** Course director: Levente Littvay (CEU Democracy Institute)

Summer and Winter Schools

- **Summer School, 10–19 July, 2022. Making Ukraine Visible—Images, Narratives, Institutions.** CEU Budapest campus and Ukrainian Catholic University campus, Lviv
- **Winter School, 21–29 January, 2023. Evidence and Truth—Reflecting on the War in Ukraine in a Global Context.** CEU Budapest campus
- **Summer School, 30 June–10 July, 2023. Cultural Representation, Decolonization, and Canon-Building: Ukraine before and after 2022.** CEU Budapest campus and Center for Urban History, Lviv
- **Winter School, 21–27 January 2024. Action and Reflection: Ukrainian Engagements with Global Knowledge Production.** CEU Budapest campus
- **Summer School, 29 June–9 July 2024. Gaining Voice in Time of War: Debate Culture, Media, and Institutions in Post-February 2022 Ukraine and Beyond.** CEU Budapest campus and Center for Urban History, Lviv

Contributors

Liana Blikharska, from Zhovkva, is writing her dissertation at the Ukrainian Catholic University and tries to understand how people create ideas and live with them. She considers the word "obvious" highly problematic and thinks that details in war can easily get lost in the shuffle.

Nadiia Chervinska, from Kolomyia, is a philosophy and history graduate who wants to believe that care, empathy, and support will one day become more powerful than military weapons.

Marta Haiduchok, from Lviv, is a PhD researcher in history at CEU. She wrote her text not because she wanted to but despite her wish never to do so. Marta's mother agrees with her essay fully.

Sasha Kokhan, from Kharkiv and Kyiv, is now studying social anthropology in Vienna. She hopes that in a couple of years, her present predictions will seem incorrect and excessively pessimistic.

Sasha Korobeinikov, from Kikvidze, is a PhD candidate in history at CEU and is currently researching Russian colonialism, imperialism, and decolonization at Freie Universität Berlin. Although he maintains an overall optimistic outlook, he is skeptical about the prospects for global democratic development in the near future.

Ela Kwiecińska, from Warsaw, is a historian and social scientist who taught modern Ukrainian and Polish history at the Faculty of History, University of Warsaw, from 2022 to 2024. She has worked at IUFU since the beginning of April 2022. Ela keeps reflecting on the limits of solidarity and the position of a non-Ukrainian bystander.

Guillaume Lancereau, from Paris, studied history and sociology in Paris, Princeton, and Florence. Since 2022, he has not been sure how to answer the question, "What are you working on?" He is still struggling with the idea that humans would need war or death to understand things differently and undertake anything new.

katia lysenko has departed from and is eternally returning to poltava, although now she studies philosophy in leipzig.

katia believes there will be no "after" the war in her life. katia tries to record the contemporaneity that is yet to come and holds on to the future that has come already.

Kateryna Osypchuk, from Kyiv, is a history major focused on the intersection of collective memory and urban studies. She reflects on how the war transformed the sense of belonging and how this, in turn, affects understanding and articulating the war. She wishes that a different cause would have strengthened these community bonds.

Oleksii Rudenko, from Mykolaiv, is a private first class of the Armed Forces of Ukraine and a PhD candidate in comparative history at the Central European University, currently on academic leave. In his first and probably last publication of 2024, Oleksii wants to evoke the classics: *Ceterum censeo Moscoviam delendam esse.*

Ostap Sereda, from Lviv, teaches modern history at the Ukrainian Catholic University, Central European University, and Bard College Berlin. He is also a coorganizer of IUFU. He is concerned about the multiple long-lasting effects of the war.

Nataliia Shuliakova, from Odesa, studied history in Vienna. Currently, she lives between Kyiv and New Haven, pursuing her studies in memory politics and urban history. She believes that the hardest thing during the war is to preserve humanness and that love doesn't die after people do.

Maksym Snihyr, from Kyiv, is a PhD researcher at Kyiv-Mohyla Academy, currently based in Regensburg. For a long time, Maksym considered himself an expat rather than part of the diaspora, but as the war drags on, he feels the increasing severance of his ties with home.

Olha Stasiuk, from Vinnytsia, is a PhD researcher in medieval studies at CEU and a cofounder of the Stasiuk Foundation that provides help to military hospitals and combat medics on the front line. For Olha, caring in this war means to remember that everyone might be in more pain than you; it means being aware of one's responsibility for the historical period and that fighting is a choice.

Denys Tereshchenko, from Poltava, studied political science in Kyiv and history in Vienna and is now beginning his PhD program at the European University Institute, Florence. Since the first week of the full-scale invasion, Denys has believed this war will last forever.

Balázs Trencsényi, from Budapest, is a Professor at the History Department of CEU in Vienna, the director of CEU's Institute for Advanced Study in Budapest, and a coorganizer of IUFU. He wishes we could have launched such an invisible university not as a response to the war but merely for intellectual pleasure.

Diána Vonnák, from Budapest, is a social anthropologist based in Scotland at the University of Stirling. She has worked in Ukraine since 2015. Initially, she wanted to understand how people cope with the heritage of past wars and collapsed political projects, but history caught up with her.

Yevhen Yashchuk, from Zhytomyr, studied history at five universities and spent his days helping at humanitarian centers and his nights coordinating students at IUFU before starting his PhD at Oxford. He observes the humanities' reluctance to critically approach the war-affected world, the emergence of new possibilities at the price of death, and the growing demand for actions with little time to evaluate them.

Tetiana Zemliakova, from Poltava, studied political science and history in Kyiv, Cambridge, and Florence. After the invasion, she focused on the ontology of time and IUFU. She always knew she was living through the last days of historical humankind, but she could never guess these would be so stupid.

Students of IUFU participating in the 2023 Budapest summer school, around the sculpture of Taras Shevchenko.

IUFU students and instructors participating in the 2024 Budapest summer school inside a Central European University lecture hall.

www.ingramcontent.com/pod-product-compliance
Ingram Content Group UK Ltd.
Pitfield, Milton Keynes, MK11 3LW, UK
UKHW042058250325
456722UK00002B/190